PLAY DRUMS NOW 2.2: RHYTHMS AND TIMING

~ TOTAL RHYTHMIC TRAINING ~

- **Skill Level:** LEVEL 2
  (prerequisite: 'Play Drums Now 1.0: DRUMSET SKILL BASICS')
  (highly recommended: Play Drums Now 2.1)

- **Estimated Time To Master This Book:**
  1-2 months (with regular practice)

- **Goals / Expected Results:**
  Well-rounded knowledge and training of rhythms and metronome use, plus increased rhythmic vocabulary.

- **Next Steps After Completing This Book:**
  COMPLETE LEVEL 2 training, with these books:

  - "PLAY DRUMS NOW 2.1: SPORT / RUDIMENTS"
  - **"PLAY DRUMS NOW 2.2: RHYTHMS + TIMING"**
  - "PLAY DRUMS NOW 2.3: DRUMSET GROOVES"
  - "PLAY DRUMS NOW 2.4: FILLS + DRUM LOOPS"
  - "PLAY DRUMS NOW 2.5: PLAYING WITH SONGS"

THEN... PROCEED TO LEVEL 3 MATERIALS!

TABLE OF CONTENTS

- RHYTHM INFO + READING - p.4
- METRONOME INFO AND EXERCISES - p.14

  ~ RHYTHM EXERCISES ~

- (INSTRUCTIONS) - p.20
- **PART I: 8TH NOTE FEEL - P.21**
- **PART II: 8TH TRIPLET FEEL - P.26**
- **PART III: 16TH NOTE FEEL - P.33**
- **PART IV: 6/8 TIME FEEL - P.40**
- **PART V: 16TH TRIPLET FEEL - P.46**
- **PART VI: SWUNG 16TH FEEL - P. 49**
- **PART VII: 32ND NOTE FEEL - P.52**

- OUTRO / NEXT STEPS - p.55

© 2021 by Adam Randall

All rights reserved. No part of this publication may be reproduced in any form without written permission of the publisher.

ISBN: 9780984436569

www.playdrumsnow.com

THIS BOOK WAS DESIGNED TO BE **THE BEST POSSIBLE TRAINING** FOR ITS PURPOSE, WITH **CAREFULLY CHOSEN** EXERCISES AND INFORMATION.

USED PROPERLY, **THIS BOOK WILL FUNDAMENTALLY ENHANCE YOUR PLAYING.**
~
PLEASE ENJOY THIS BOOK!
-ADAM RANDALL

INSTRUCTIONS FOR THIS BOOK

1) Do your best!

2) Read all the instructions carefully.

3) STAY IN CONTROL (avoid mistakes).

4) Prioritize sound quality.

5) Practice with focus, like you're training for a SPORT.

6) Rehearse patterns thoroughly, like you're memorizing a LANGUAGE.

7) Go generally in order from beginning to end in this book.

8) USE www.PlayDrumsNow.com for more resources.

PLAY DRUMS NOW
THE ULTIMATE DRUMSET TRAINING PROGRAM

USE PROPER TECHNIQUE

- **Stay relaxed**
- **Use wrist control (not arms)**
- **Keep palms down and elbows at sides**

<u>FOR MORE SPECIFICS ON TECHNIQUE</u>:

- 'Play Drums Now 1.0: Drumset Skill Basics'
- 'Play Drums Now 2.1: Sport / Rudiments'

All the exercises in the 'Play Drums Now' books are split up into the 4 'most typical musical feels'.

This is because almost 100% of modern music falls into one of these four categories - so as a drummer, it's strategic to **train your skills in all of them so you can be fully versatile.**

16TH NOTE FEEL

pulses grouped 4 at a time:

| o o o o | o o o o | o o o o | o o o o |
  1 e & a   **2** e & a   **3** e & a   **4** e & a

8TH TRIPLET FEEL

pulses grouped 3 at a time:

| o o o | o o o | o o o | o o o |
  1 & a   **2** & a   **3** & a   **4** & a

6/8 TIME FEEL

pulses grouped 6 at a time:

| o o o o o o | o o o o o o |
  1 & 2 & 3 & **4** & 5 & 6 &

SWUNG 16TH FEEL

pulses grouped in a 'shuffle':

|o _ oo _ o|o _ oo _ o|o _ oo _ o|o _ oo _ o|
 1 _ e&_ a **2** _ e&_ a **3** _ e&_ a **4** _ e&_ a

Find example songs in each feel on Spotify, by searching these playlists:

'**DRUMS 16th feel**'   '**DRUMS Swung16th feel**'
'**DRUMS 8th triplet feel**'   '**DRUMS 6/8 time feel**'

READING THE NOTATION IN THIS BOOK

All exercises in this book use this key:

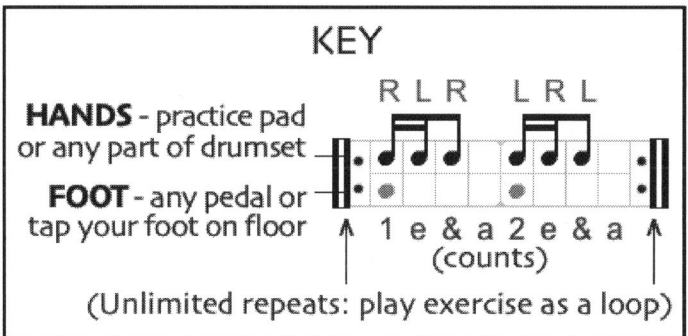

THE GRID / STAFF

This is used to make it easy to see the spacing of the rhythms in music.

UNLIMITED REPEATS

Repeat/loop the pattern as many times as you want without stopping. (Usually repeat signs mean 'play the section twice, then continue on'.)

(R,L) -> (L,R) ->

These symbols indicate alternating sticking, starting with the indicated side. When both are listed, practice each individually until they are both easy.

THE ORIGIN OF RHYTHM

All rhythms start with the universal grid of CONSTANT PULSES. Different rhythms come from:

- grouping these pulses by 3,4,6, etc.
- removing some of the pulses.
- setting a specific tempo for the pulses.

PULSE RHYTHM
|o o o o o o o o o o o o|

PULSE RHYTHM (grouped 3 pulses at a time)
|o o o|o o o|o o o|o o o|

PULSE RHYTHM (grouped 4 pulses at a time)
|o o o o|o o o o|o o o o|

RHYTHM "A" (some pulses removed)
|o o _ o _ _ o o o _ o _|

RHYTHM "A" (grouped 3 pulses at a time)
|o o _|o _ _|o o o|_ o _|

RHYTHM "A" (grouped 4 pulses at a time)
|o o _ o|_ _ o o|o _ o _|

'PULSE RHYTHMS' ARE THE RHYTHMIC BACKDROP FOR EVERYTHING IN MUSIC.

Musicians use an agreed-upon PULSE RHYTHM as the guideline for the timing of all notes in a song.

They decide on **the speed of pulses ('tempo')** and **how the pulses are grouped.**

Everyone playing notes in correlation with the same pulse rhythm will be 'in sync' and the music will sound aligned.

GROUPING PULSES 3, 4, OR 6 AT A TIME CREATES THE 'FOUR MOST TYPICAL MUSICAL FEELS'.

These groups of pulses are known as **'beats'.**

A rhythm will feel different each time it is grouped in a different way. (see examples of RHYTHM "A", bottom left).

EACH 'FEEL' OF MUSIC IS ACCOMPANIED BY ITS OWN SYSTEM OF COUNTING.

This helps in vocalizing the counts, so musicians have something steady to play rhythms against, as well as a way to talk about specific locations in a measure.

THESE FOUR FEELS can account for ~99% of popular music, so as a drummer, it's worth learning to read and play music (rhythms, grooves, fills, and songs) in each feel.

THE FOUR MOST TYPICAL FEELS OF MUSIC

AND THEIR COUNTING SYSTEMS:

When you group steady pulses 4 per beat:

| o o o o | o o o o | o o o o | o o o o |

  1 e & a   **2** e & a   **3** e & a   **4** e & a

This is considered the **'16th note feel'** and is counted vocally as shown above, with **four pulses per 'beat'**.

 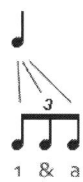

If you group the pulses 3 at a time:

| o o o | o o o | o o o | o o o |

  1 & a   **2** & a   **3** & a   **4** & a

This is considered the **'8th triplet feel'** and is usually counted as shown, with **three pulses per 'beat'**.

EXAMPLES OF EACH FEEL

There are Spotify playlists specific to each feel, where you can find plenty of song examples.

Visit: www.playdrumsnow.com/tempos/

Grouping pulses into 6 at a time:

| o o o o o o | o o o o o o |

  1 & 2 & 3 & **4** & 5 & 6 &

This is considered the **'6/8 feel'** and is usually counted as shown, with **six pulses per 'beat'**.

Grouping pulses into 6 at a time, but omitting some of the counts to make a 'shuffle' rhythm:

| o _ o o _ o | o _ o o _ o | o _ o o _ o |

  1 _ e& _ a   **2** _ e& _ a   **3** _ e& _ a

This is considered the **'swung 16th feel'** and is usually counted as shown, with **four (swung) pulses per 'beat'**.

WRITTEN RHYTHMIC LANGUAGE

'RHYTHM NOTATION'

This is a system of 'notes' and 'rests' of various sizes, that can **represent any rhythm**.

Just learn what all the pieces are, and use a little math to combine them properly inside measures.

THE BASIC RULE OF WRITING RHYTHMS is:

every measure must be filled completely with notes and rests so the rhythm can be interpreted correctly.

This system is helpful because the rhythm is always clear, and the notes don't have to be spaced perfectly.

NOTES + RESTS ARE THE 'ALPHABET' OF THE LANGUAGE

Be familiar with these figures and learn how to tell them apart.

THE FOLLOWING PAGE shows all the various notes/rests,* with their lengths represented by the grey bars behind them.

The APPEARANCE is described on the left, and explains how to tell the sizes apart.

*(whole notes aren't shown because the scale would have to be smaller, plus drummers rarely use them.)

HOW NOTES MAKE BEATS

Once these note and rest 'bricks' are packed next to each other within a measure, they are usually **connected within each beat.**

This generally makes reading the rhythms much easier, **like reading words on a page,** instead of only letters at a time.

'FLAGS' (SINGLE) AND 'BEAMS' (CONNECTED)

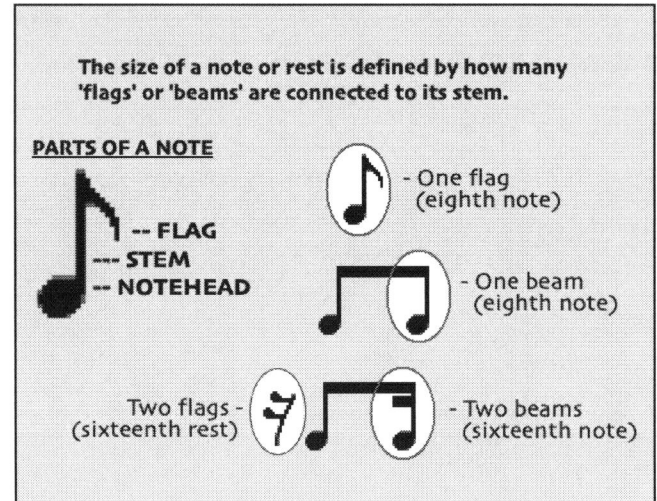

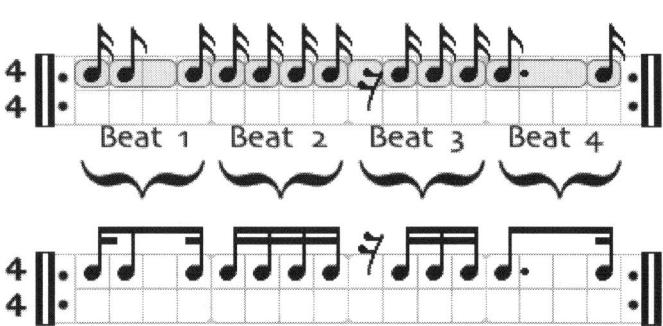

RHYTHMIC ALPHABET

Get to know these pieces!

NOTES AND RESTS are measured as fractions of a 'whole note' (not shown) - just like fractions of an inch on a ruler.

(Dotted notes are 150% ("three halves") the size of regular notes.)

> **'Triplet' notes** are 3 evenly spaced notes/rests in the area that only 2 would normally fit. These are designated by a '3' displayed over the notes/rests. (It's also possible to create 'quintuplets', 'sextuplets', and other '-tuplets' by adding other numbers over a group of notes.

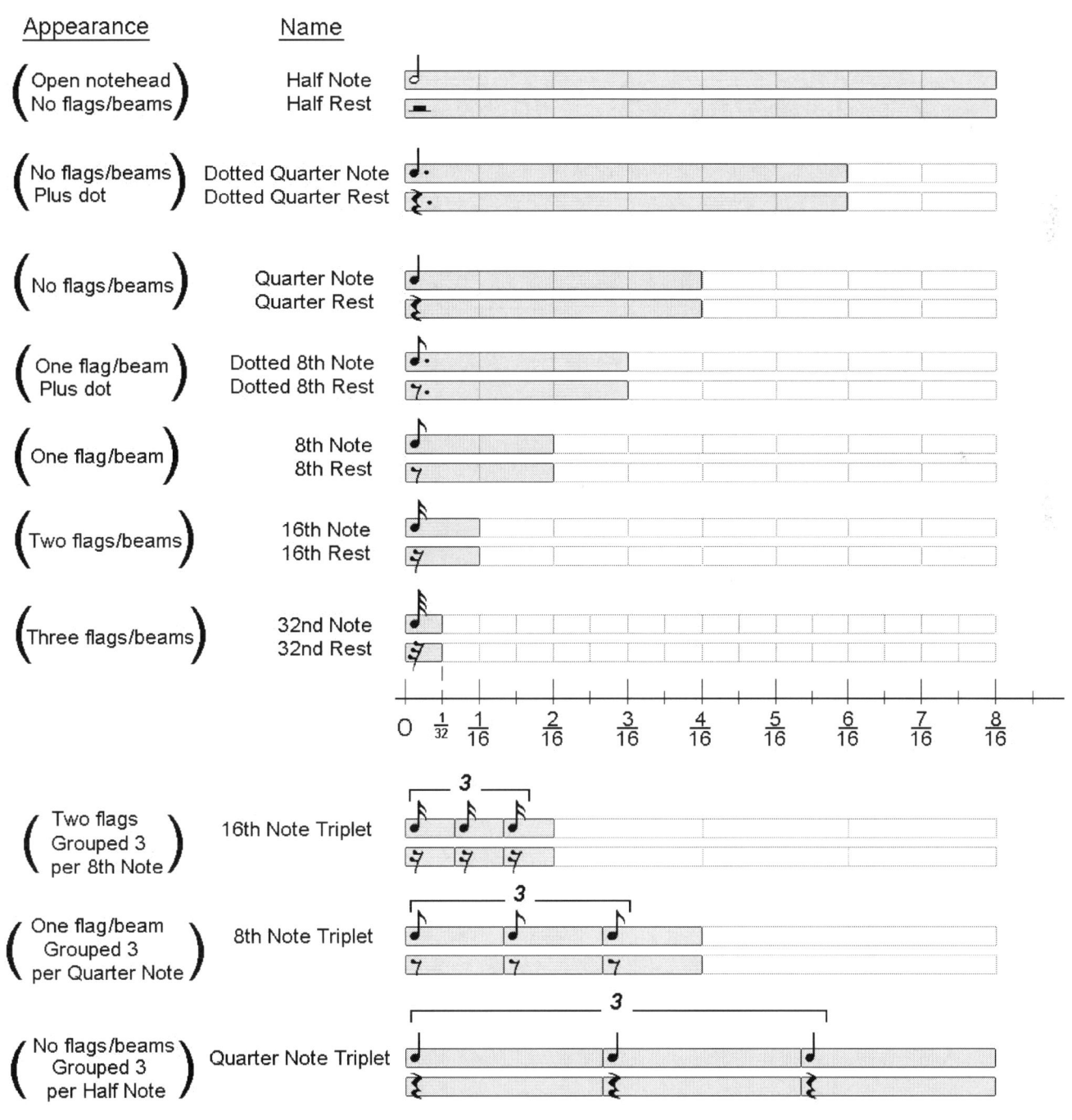

RHYTHM VOCABULARY

Try to familiarize yourself with as many of these as you can, to make reading music easier.

16th-note figures (16 total)

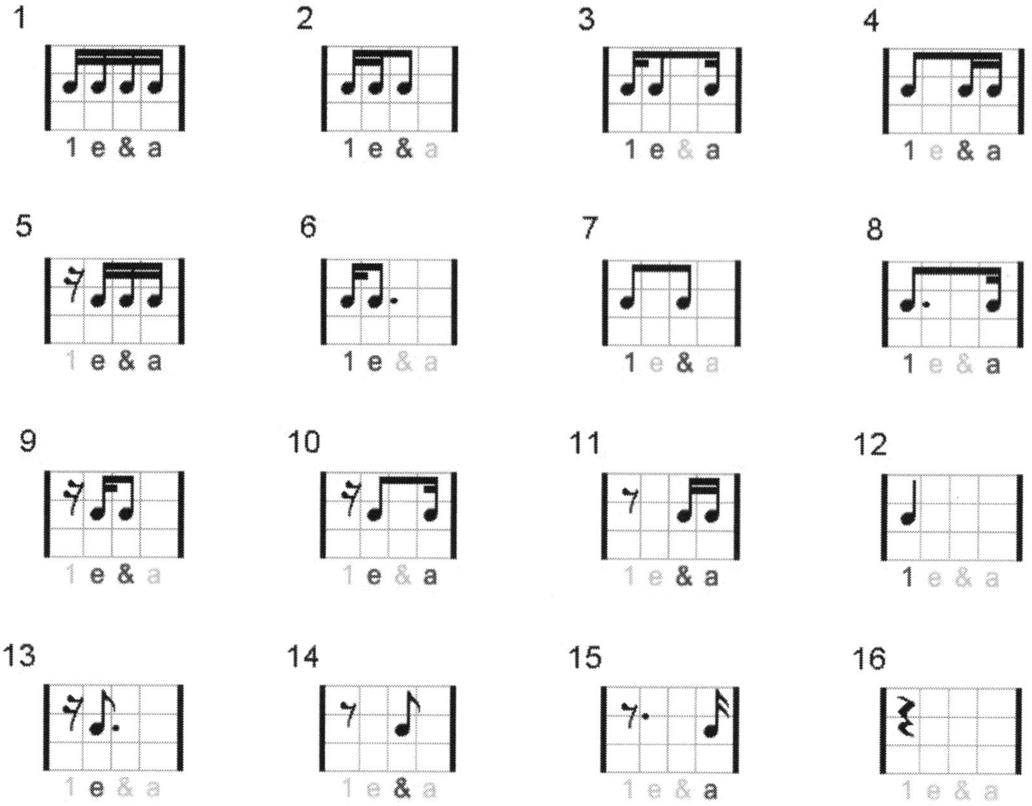

1
1 e & a

2
1 e & a

3
1 e & a

4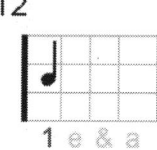
1 e & a

5
1 e & a

6
1 e & a

7
1 e & a

8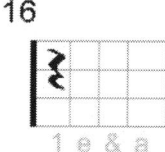
1 e & a

9
1 e & a

10
1 e & a

11
1 e & a

12
1 e & a

13
1 e & a

14
1 e & a

15
1 e & a

16
1 e & a

Common 32nd-note figures (65 total)

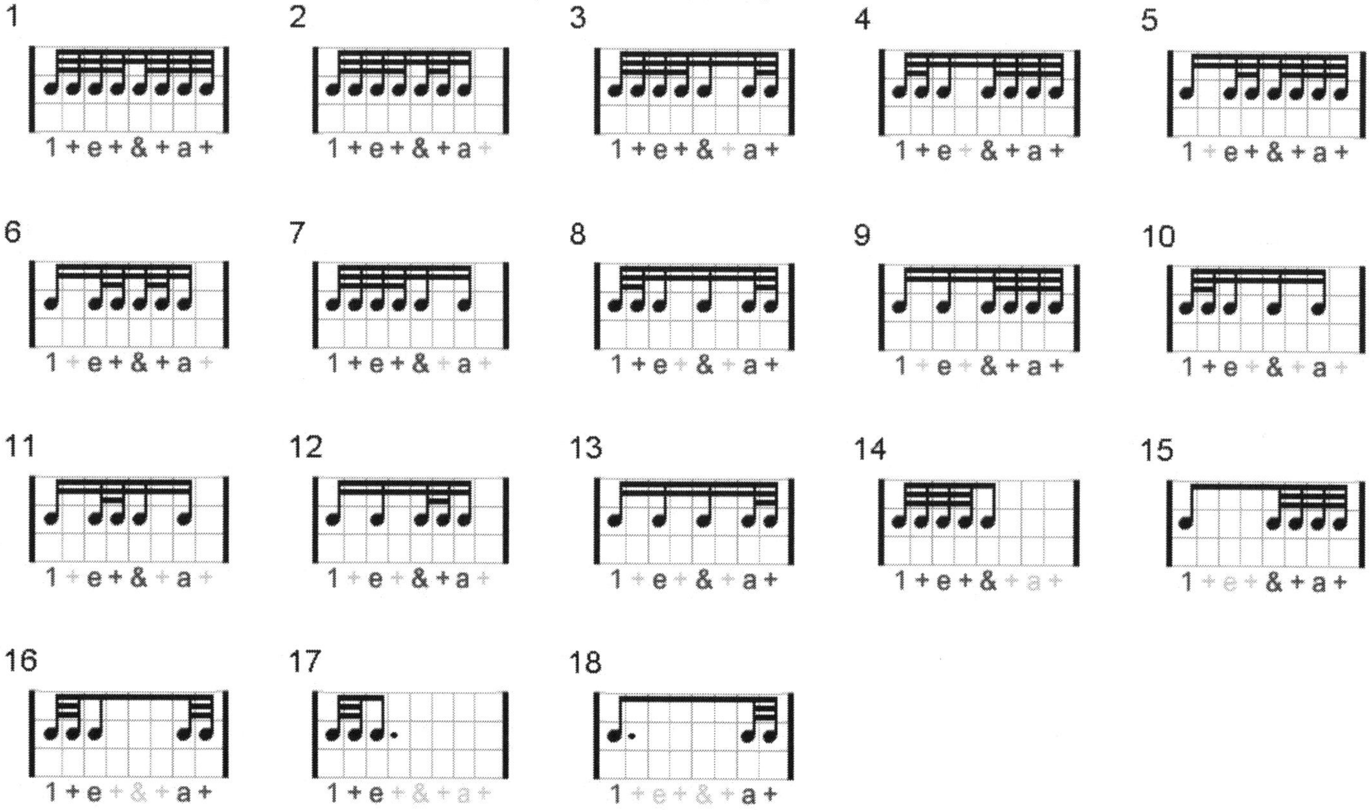

1
1 + e + & + a +

2
1 + e + & + a +

3
1 + e + & + a +

4
1 + e + & + a +

5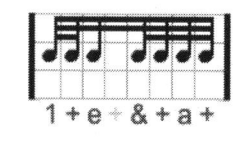
1 + e + & + a +

6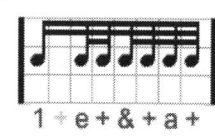
1 + e + & + a +

7
1 + e + & + a +

8
1 + e + & + a +

9
1 + e + & + a +

10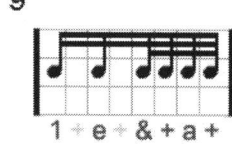
1 + e + & + a +

11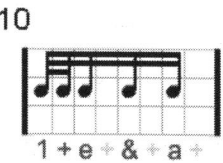
1 + e + & + a +

12
1 + e + & + a +

13
1 + e + & + a +

14
1 + e + & + a +

15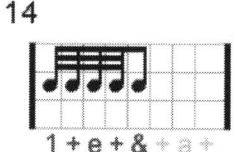
1 + e + & + a +

16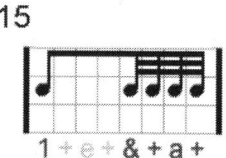
1 + e + & + a +

17
1 + e + & + a +

18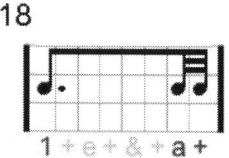
1 + e + & + a +

8th-triplet figures (8 total)

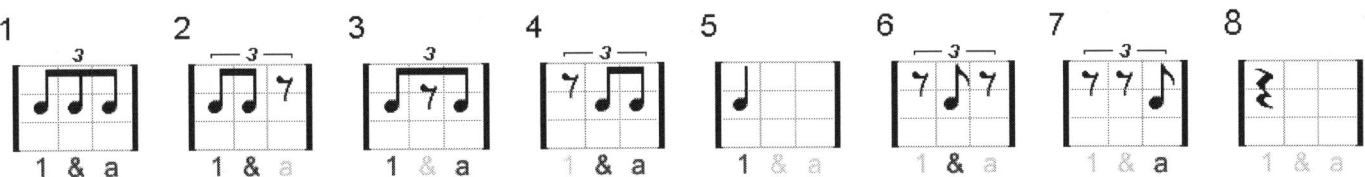

Common 16th-note figures in 6/8 time (64 total)

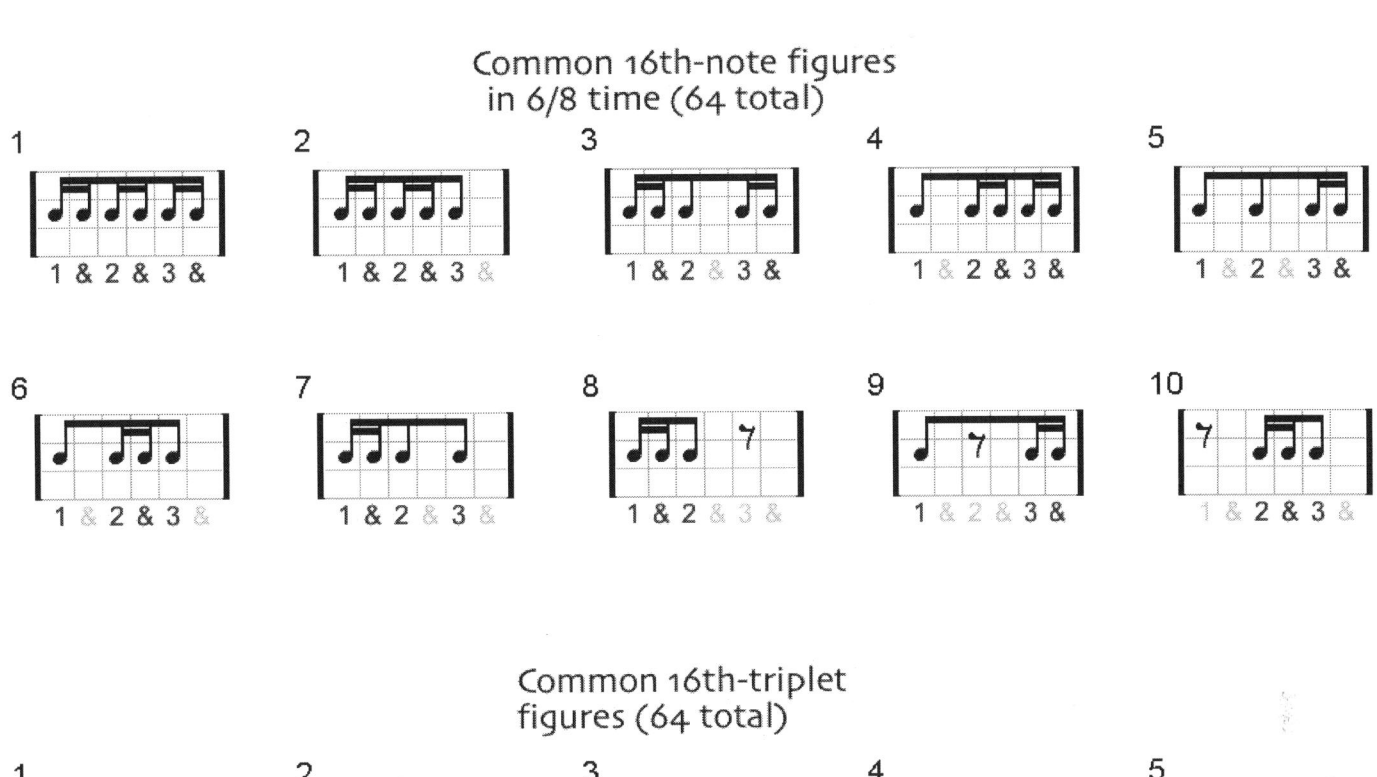

Common 16th-triplet figures (64 total)

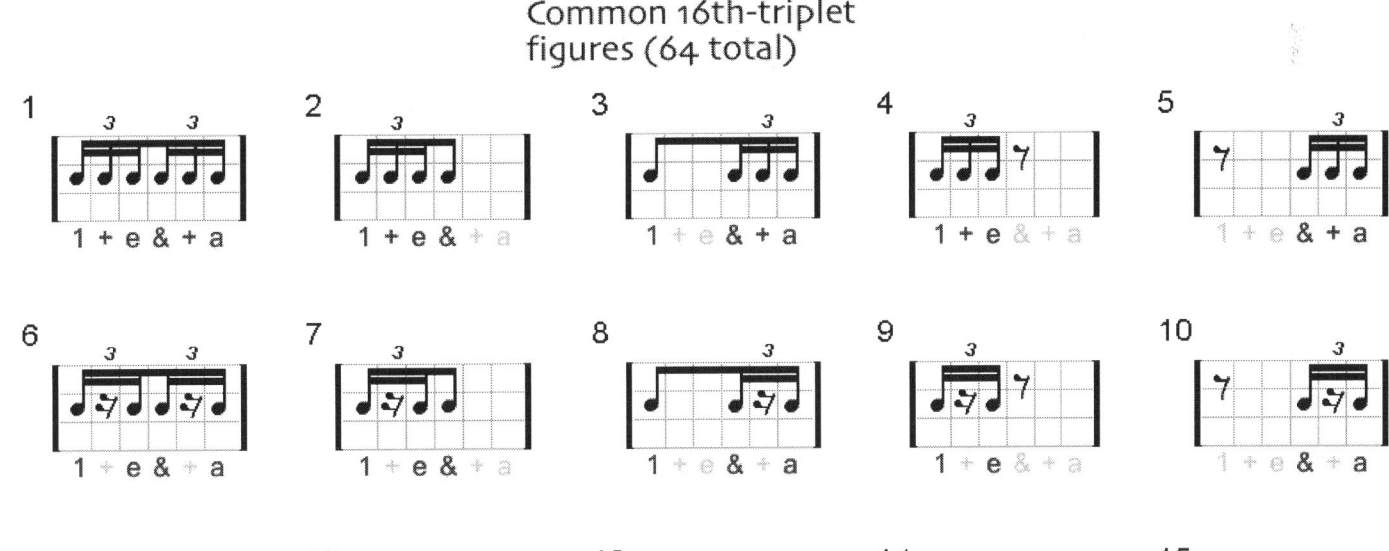

ANATOMY OF MEASURES

Measures serve as **building blocks** for arranging songs. Each major section of a song (i.e. 'verse', 'chorus', 'bridge', etc.) is usually a solid number of measures.

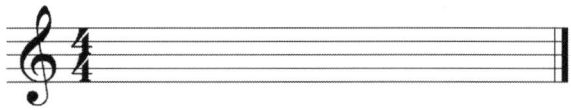

THE LENGTH OF A MEASURE IS ITS 'TIME SIGNATURE'.

Measure length is described by a **certain number of quarter notes, eighth notes, or 16th notes.**

<u>The bottom number</u> of the time signature indicates the note-type used as the unit of length **(4=quarter note, 8=8th note, 16=16th note).**

<u>The top number</u> tells you how many of those notes would fit into the measure.

For example, the following time signature is called **'3-4 time'** and indicates that the measures in the music are **three quarter-notes long.**

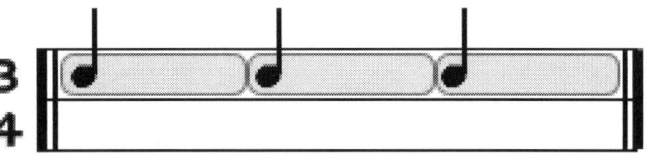

THIS time signature is called **'5-16 time'** and indicates that the measures in the music are **five sixteenth-notes long.**

Measure size influences the FEEL.

Certain sizes of measures are only compatible with some 'feels' - for example, a 5/8-time measure can be used for the 16th note feel or swung 16th feel, but not an 8th triplet feel (which requires a solid number of quarter notes, one for each triplet).

Some common time signatures are shown on the following page. >>

TYPICAL TIME SIGNATURES

Many other measure sizes are possible too, such as 5/16, 7/4, 13/8, etc.

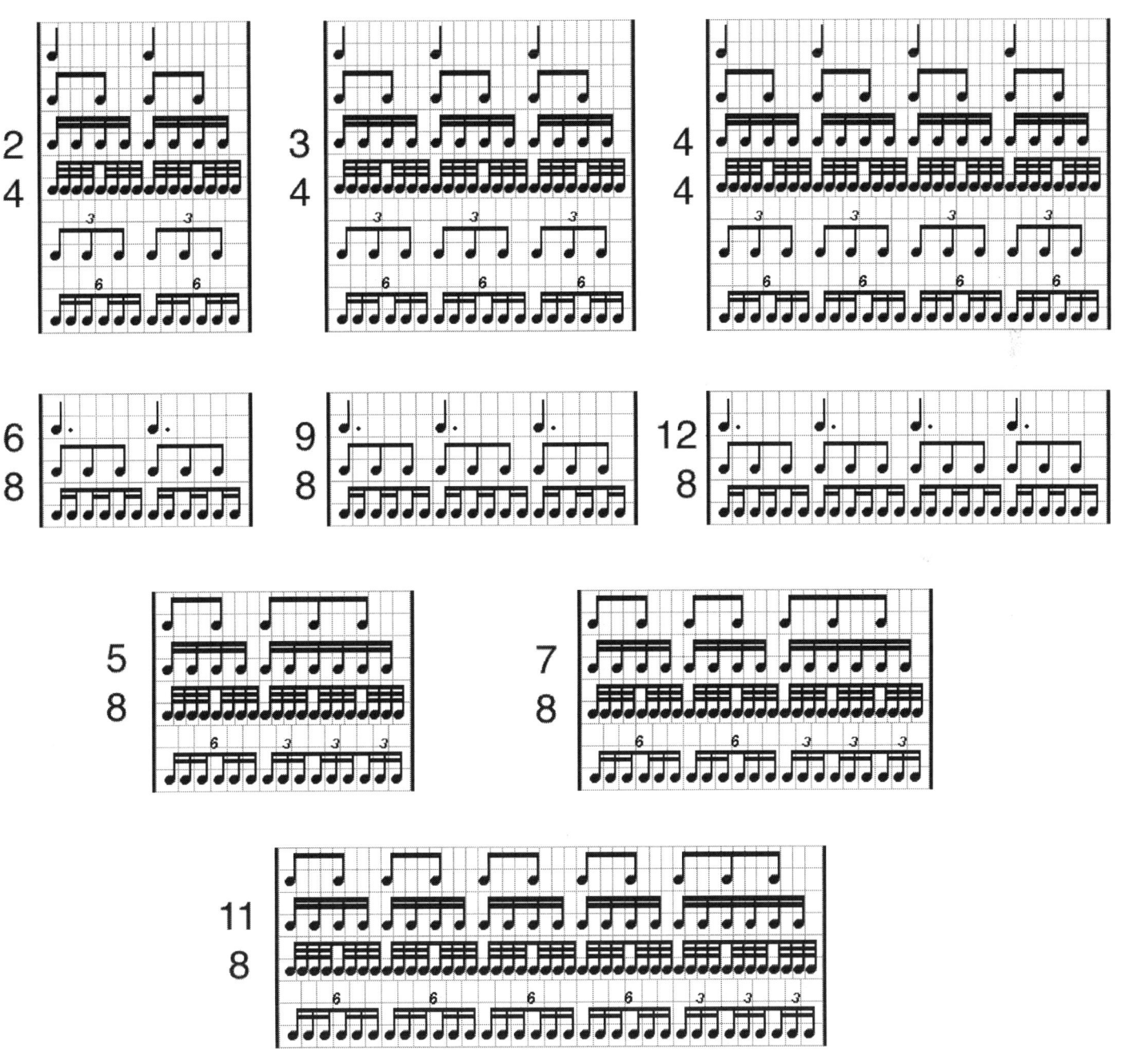

BENEFITS OF PRACTICING RHYTHMS

THERE ARE THREE MAIN SKILL BENEFITS FROM PRACTICING WITH RHYTHMS:

1) ACCURATE TIMING SKILLS

- **When your timing is really sharp and consistent**, you will be highly respected by the musicians around you.

  And as the timing quality of parts within music improves, the music will feel more 'alive'!

- **Practice playing everything in this book with a metronome** (at various speeds), because you'll be doing your timing skills a giant favor.

  Not to mention your reading skills!

- **The rhythms in this book cover almost every type of rhythmic territory,** with a variety of examples in each, to help you be a more versatile drummer.

2) READING MUSIC NOTATION

Often, drummers are tempted to overlook this skill and think of it like a time-consuming hindrance to their progress.

It is actually a vital skill.

- **Learning to read rhythms greatly accelerates your progress as a drummer!** When you understand written patterns, you can learn any of the written grooves, fills, songs, etc., you come across in books or on the internet.

  You'll be able to expand your vocabulary way more rapidly by learning written music than by trying to imitate and memorize things you hear.

- **Reading drumset notation starts with reading rhythms.** Practice reading the music in this book until you can understand it fluently, then drumset notation will be fairly easy to read - it's really just rhythms phrased on different parts of a drumset.

- **Writing music is important too!** With practice, you'll even be able to document the brilliant ideas that come to you during practice.

3) YOUR 'RHYTHMIC VOCABULARY'

- **In music, 'vocabulary' refers to ideas that you can PLAY as well as REMEMBER.**
  You want to be able to execute any of your vocabulary on command, so you can effortlessly draw from a bank of ideas when you play drums.

> RHYTHMIC VOCABULARY IS THE MOST IMPORTANT TYPE OF MUSICAL VOCABULARY.

- **RHYTHMS are the true foundation** of all grooves, fills, songs... EVERY musical expression is just a rhythm phrased on different sounds or different notes.

- **Generally, the more rhythms you know, the more creative you can be.** You can easily invent a groove or fill when you think of a rhythm first, then adapt it to the format of 'groove' or 'fill'.

- Part of what helps develop your vocabulary is to make sure you <u>look away from the music while playing each rhythm</u>, to ensure that it's in your memory before going to the next one.

> This book includes all the major 'rhythm types' so you can get used to reading them all, so you'll understand any music you come across.

Ways to incorporate RHYTHMS into your practice routine:

- Spend part of each practice session playing rhythms on a practice pad (improve your technique and timing)

- Choose one rhythm at a time and play it as a FILL on the drumset - find several ways to make it sound good

USING A METRONOME

Before practicing with rhythms, you will need to be familiar using this tool.

TRAINING FOR YOUR SENSE OF TIMING

Metronome /ˈme.trəˌnoʊm/ noun [C]:
A machine that plays steady pulses of sound.

Uses / PURPOSE: helps you train your internal sense of timing, and calibrate your playing to be sure it's steady.

HOW TO SET A METRONOME:

Metronomes all have some typical settings:

- **TEMPO** (speed in 'beats per minute')
- **VOLUME**
- **SOUND TYPE** (beeps, clicks, etc.)
- **TIME SIGNATURE** (a.k.a. measure length; requires an 'accent pulse' or 'first beat' sound to make it relevant)
- **SUBDIVISION NOTES** (faster pulses with a different sound than the main 'beat' pulse, that divide it into groups of 2,3,4, 6, etc.).

These last two important settings will together determine **the 'feel'** of the rhythm and music.

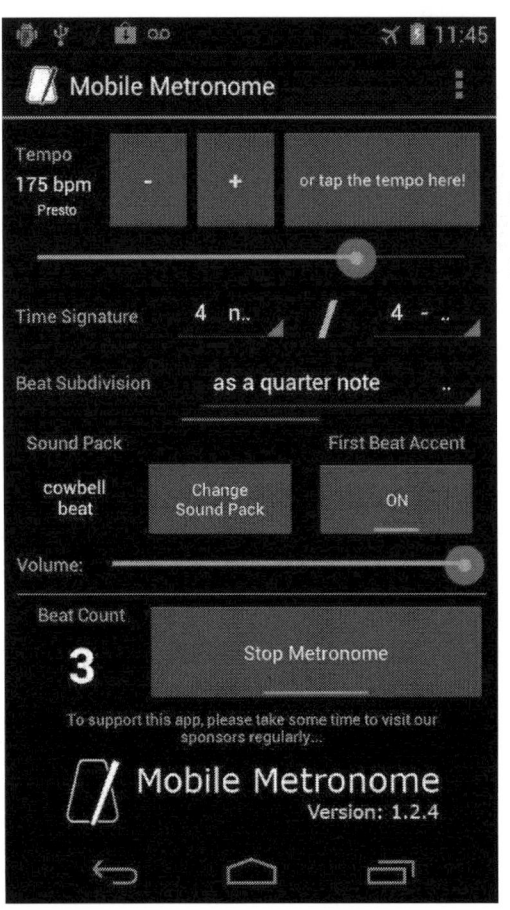

(screenshot of a typical metronome << app)

YOU DECIDE WHAT IT MEANS

When a metronome is playing constant steady pulses (without an audible 'time signature' or 'subdivision' pulse), **you can decide how to group the pulses** - whether you think of them in groups of 3,4,6, or a different size determines the 'feel' of the metronome. Try it out!

The 'time signature' and 'beat subdivision' settings just make it easier to hear certain feels.

EXERCISE 1: SETTING THE METRONOME TO EACH FEEL

A: 16TH NOTE FEEL, 4/4 TIME

- START AT A **TEMPO of 80 bpm** and hit PLAY.

- SET THE **TIME SIGNATURE** (a.k.a. measure length) to '4 beats' or '4/4 time', whichever is an option.

- SET THE **SUBDIVISION NOTES to '16th notes'** to hear all the pulses in the measure. Listen for a bit to internalize the sound.

- Try counting **16th note counts** '1-e-&-a...' etc. along with the metronome.

- Then, change the **subdivision setting to '8th notes'** and try to imagine the sound of the 16th notes, as if they are still playing. Then repeat this step with the setting on 'quarter notes'.

B: 8TH TRIPLET FEEL, 4/4 TIME

- START AT A **TEMPO** of 80 bpm and hit PLAY.

- SET THE **TIME SIGNATURE** (a.k.a. measure length) to '4 beats' or '4/4 time', whichever is an option.

- SET THE **SUBDIVISION NOTES** to '8th note triplets' to hear all the pulses in the measure. Listen for a bit to internalize the sound.

- Try counting **8th triplet counts** '1-&-a...' etc. along with the metronome.

- Then, change the **subdivision setting to 'quarter notes'** and try to imagine the sound of the 8th triplets, as if they are still playing.

C: 6/8 TIME FEEL, 6/8 TIME

**NOTE: These settings won't use correct note values, but they WILL sound correct.

- START AT A **TEMPO** of 120 bpm and hit PLAY.

- SET THE **TIME SIGNATURE** (a.k.a. measure length) to '3 beats' or '3/4 time', whichever is an option.

- SET THE **SUBDIVISION NOTES to '8th notes'** to hear all the pulses in the measure. Listen for a bit to internalize the sound.

- Try counting **6/8 time counts** '1-&-2-&-3-&...' etc. along with the metronome.

- Then, change the **subdivision setting to 'quarter notes'** and try to imagine the sound of the 8th notes, as if they are still playing.

D: SWUNG 16TH NOTE FEEL, 4/4 TIME

- START AT A **TEMPO** of 60 bpm and hit PLAY.

- SET THE **TIME SIGNATURE** (a.k.a. measure length) to '4 beats' or '4/4 time', whichever is an option.

- SET THE **SUBDIVISION NOTES to '16th triplet notes' or 'sextuplets'** to hear all the triplet pulses in the measure. Listen for a bit to internalize the sound.

- Try counting **swung 16th note counts** '1 - e& - a2 - e& - a...' etc. along with the metronome.

- Then, change the **subdivision setting to '8th notes'** and try to imagine the sound of the swung 16th notes, as if they are still playing. Then repeat this step with the setting on 'quarter notes'.

EXERCISE 2: PLAYING 'PULSES' WITH THE METRONOME

GOAL: Learn to imitate the metronome perfectly.

A: SUBDIVISIONS ON

- Use a practice pad and proper technique.
- FOR THE '16TH NOTE FEEL' RHYTHMS:
  - A) Set the metronome to the 'slow' setting, with **all subdivisions turned on** (i.e. 16th notes, in the '16th feel').
  - B) Play each rhythm with the metronome for ~30 sec. to 1 min.
  - C) Focus on landing every note you play at EXACTLY THE SAME TIME as the metronome 'click' you're aiming for. Your goal is to 'eclipse' its sound so you can only hear the sound of your stick.
  - D) Now try the same rhythms with the 'medium' and 'fast' settings on the metronome.
- REPEAT THESE ^^ STEPS FOR THE '8TH TRIPLET' FEEL, '6/8 TIME' FEEL, AND 'SWUNG 16TH' FEEL RHYTHMS.

B: SUBDIVISIONS OFF

- Use a practice pad and proper technique.
- FOR THE '16TH NOTE FEEL' RHYTHMS:
  - A) Set the metronome to the 'slow' setting, with **all subdivisions turned off** (quarter notes, in the '16th feel').
  - B) Play each rhythm with the metronome for ~30 sec. to 1 min.
  - C) Focus on landing every note you play at EXACTLY THE SAME TIME as the metronome 'click' you're aiming for. Your goal is to 'eclipse' its sound so you can only hear the sound of your stick.
  - D) Now try the same rhythms with the 'medium' and 'fast' settings on the metronome.
- REPEAT THESE ^^ STEPS FOR THE '8TH TRIPLET' FEEL, '6/8 TIME' FEEL, AND 'SWUNG 16TH' FEEL RHYTHMS.

Part 1: 16th Note FEEL

Metronome settings:

SLOW ♩ =80 bpm
MED ♩ =110 bpm
FAST ♩ =140+ bpm

If possible with your metronome, you can add a 'x2' (8th note) subdivision pulse, or a 'x4' (16th note) pulse to represent all the spaces in the grid.

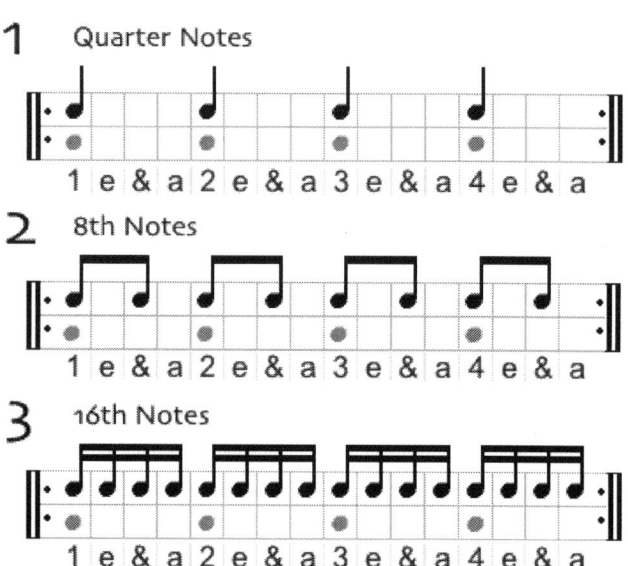

1 Quarter Notes
   1 e & a 2 e & a 3 e & a 4 e & a

2 8th Notes
   1 e & a 2 e & a 3 e & a 4 e & a

3 16th Notes
   1 e & a 2 e & a 3 e & a 4 e & a

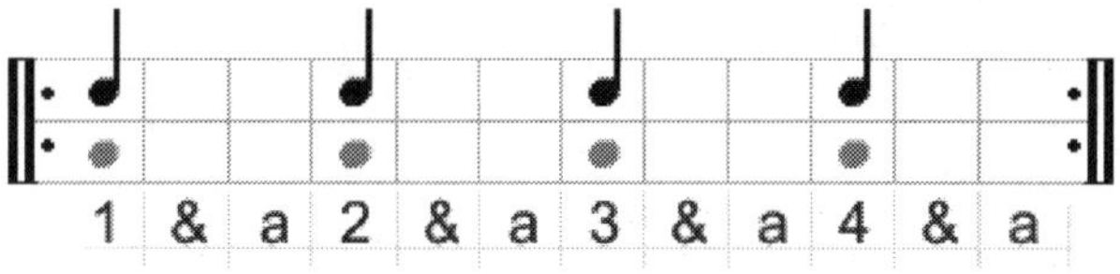

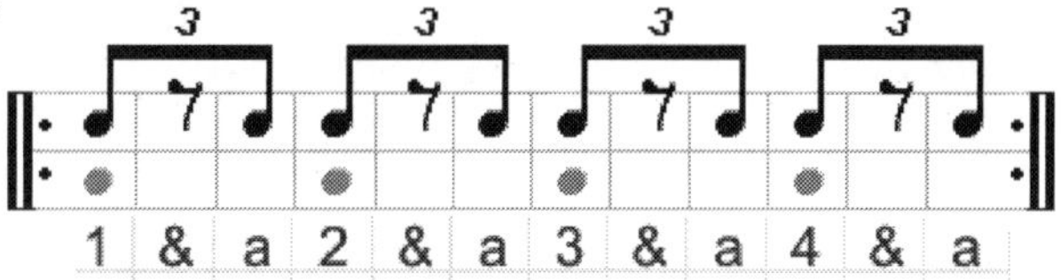

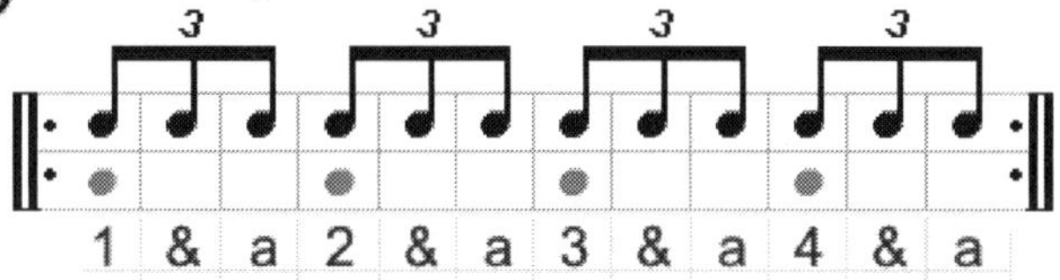

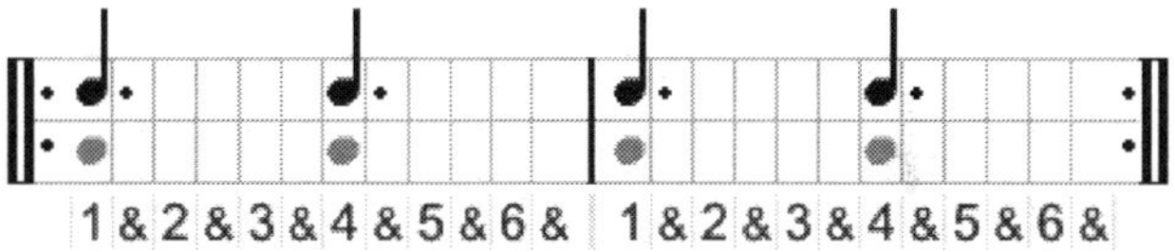

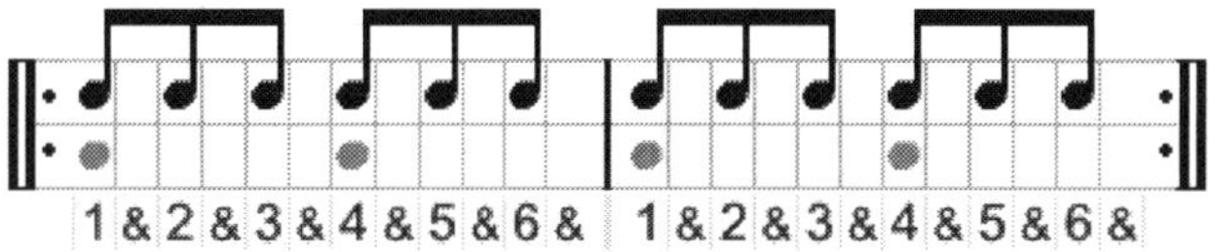

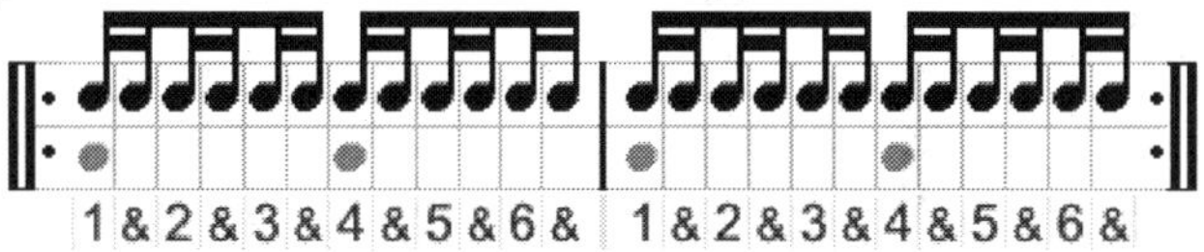

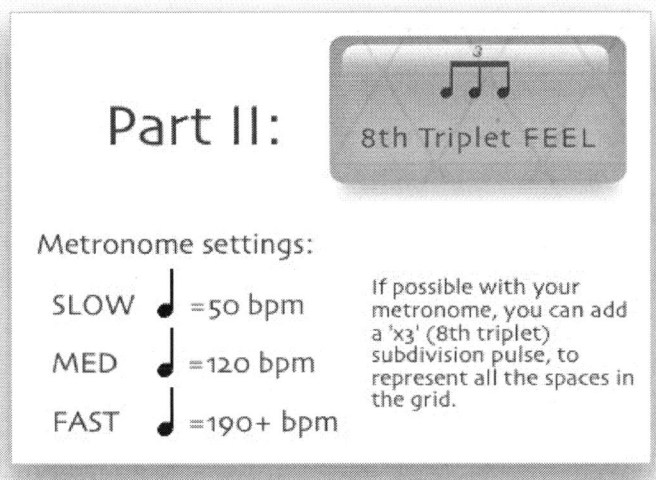
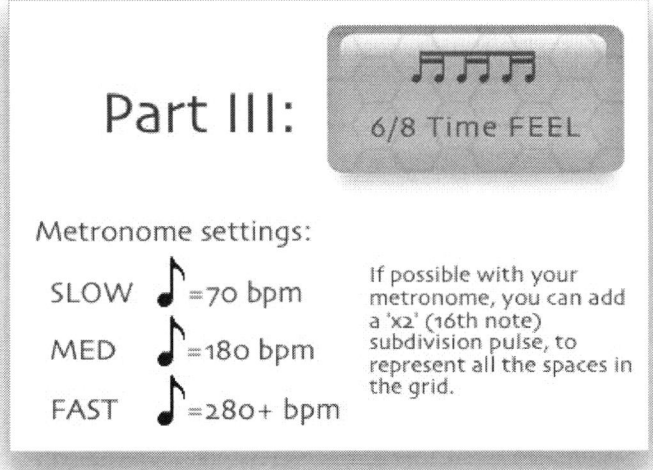
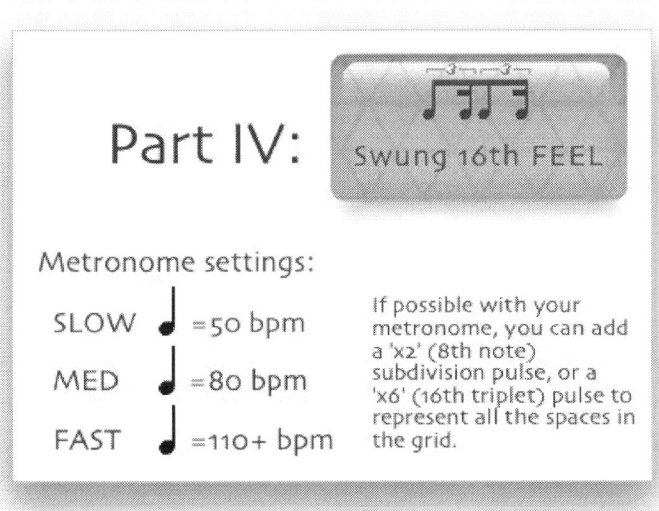

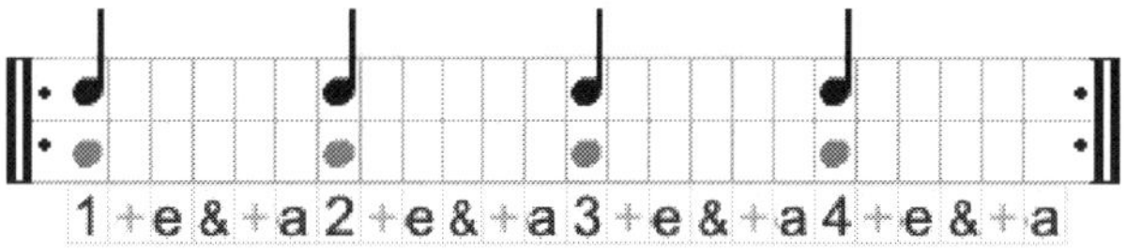

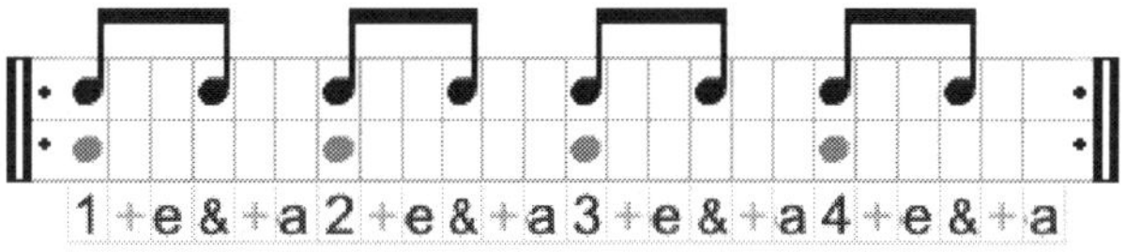

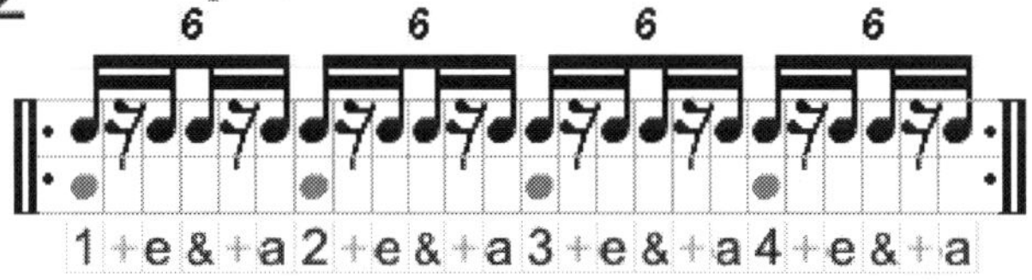

TIPS FOR LEARNING RHYTHMS

R,L STICKING PATTERNS

Your best goal is versatility.

That way, your timing doesn't depend on a certain way of playing the pattern, and you'll be able to adapt the rhythm easily to various purposes.

You can use any sequence of R/L (hands or feet) to play a rhythm, anywhere on the spectrum between using 'only one limb' and 'every limb on every note'.

START WITH ALTERNATING STROKES

The best way to play rhythms at first is with alternating strokes. There are a couple kinds of alternating:

- 'NATURAL ALTERNATING'   >>

This means switching hands for every note, regardless of what the rhythm is. <u>This is usually the best approach,</u> and tends to develop the most versatility and balance between the hands.

- 'SUBTRACTIVE ALTERNATING'   >>

(or 'dominant alternating') This means assigning R and L to alternate counts of the overall grid, and any spaces in the rhythm are **skipped without influencing the original assigned pattern.**

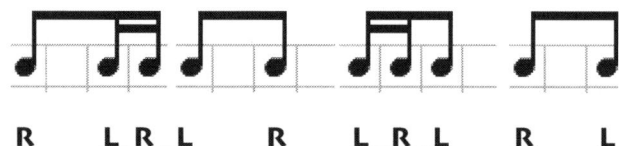

R   L R L   R   L R L   R   L

R L R L R   L R L   R L R   L   R L R

The 'leading hand' refers to whichever hand you start the pattern with.

KEEP THE COUNTING GOING

Speaking the counts in a measure while you play **serves as a personal metronome** AND helps you get used to **which part of the measure you're on**.

It's important to learn rhythms this way at first, to make sure the spacing is correct.

After lots of practice WITH counting, you'll probably have a strong internal sense of timing - and then you can just 'think' or 'feel' the counts.

> **TIP:** Even when you can remember the sound of a rhythm and 'play it by ear', it's important to **STAY AWARE of the underlying grid of pulses** to keep your timing and tempo extra accurate!
>
> Listen to your internal metronome at all times.

WATCH YOUR TECHNIQUE

Rhythms provide a great opportunity to make sure everything looks good in your physical setup. Practice staying in your ideal 'default' positioning while playing any rhythms.

Your habits of execution for rhythms will apply to every other type of drumming you do, so improvements you make to playing rhythms are valuable!

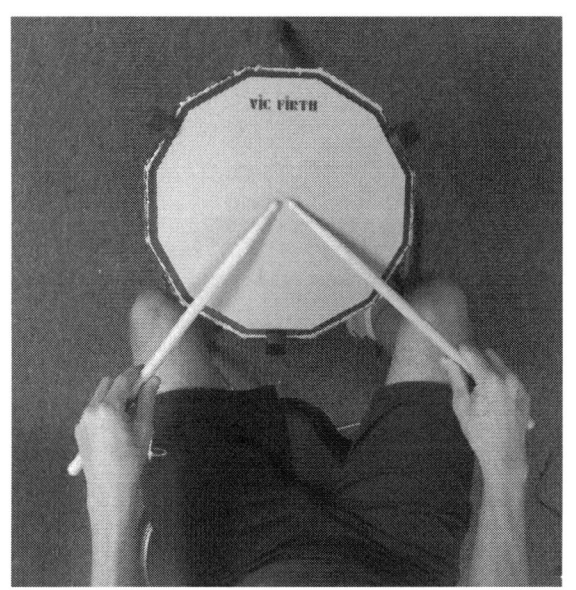

FOR MORE SPECIFICS ON TECHNIQUE:

- 'Play Drums Now 1.0: Drumset Skill Basics'
- 'Play Drums Now 2.1: Sport / Rudiments'

INSTRUCTIONS FOR UNIVERSAL RHYTHMS

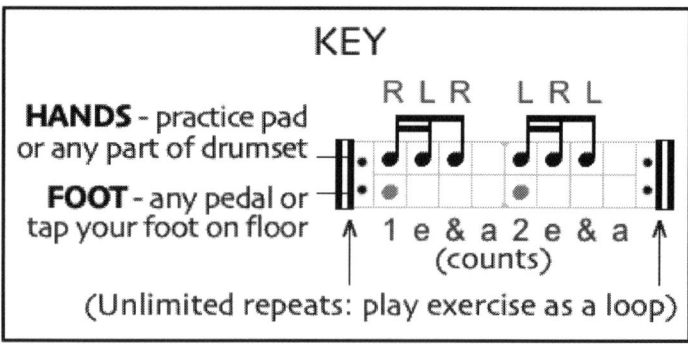

KEY

HANDS - practice pad or any part of drumset
FOOT - any pedal or tap your foot on floor

(counts)

(Unlimited repeats: play exercise as a loop)

EXERCISE 1: Learn the rhythms

Speak (or think) all the counts steadily, while you read and play each rhythm.

Make sure you can **play each at least 4 times in a row at the same tempo** (but more repetitions is always better).

EXERCISE 2: Add a metronome

Set the metronome to the 'slow' tempo, and **spend some time playing each rhythm** with it to perfect your timing. (Look away from the music as soon as you can remember the rhythm.)

Repeat this step with the metronome set to other tempos.

EXERCISE 3: Add the 'pulse note'

Use either your right or left foot for the grey pulse note on the lower line.

Play each rhythm along with the pulse note, at least 4 times in a row at the same tempo

Spend some time playing each rhythm this way at various tempos (with or without the metronome).

TIPS

- **Use any sticking (R,L) pattern** for playing the patterns
  (see p.13 for 'sticking patterns')

- **Maintain good technique**
  (closed grip and full strokes is ideal)

- **Focus on perfecting your timing** during all exercises

- Use these instructions on one section of rhythms at a time (8th note feel, 8th triplet feel, etc.)

UNIVERSAL RHYTHMS PART 1:

8th Note Feel

- 1-MEASURE LENGTH RHYTHMS - P.22
- 4-MEASURE LENGTH RHYTHMS - P.24

UNIVERSAL RHYTHMS

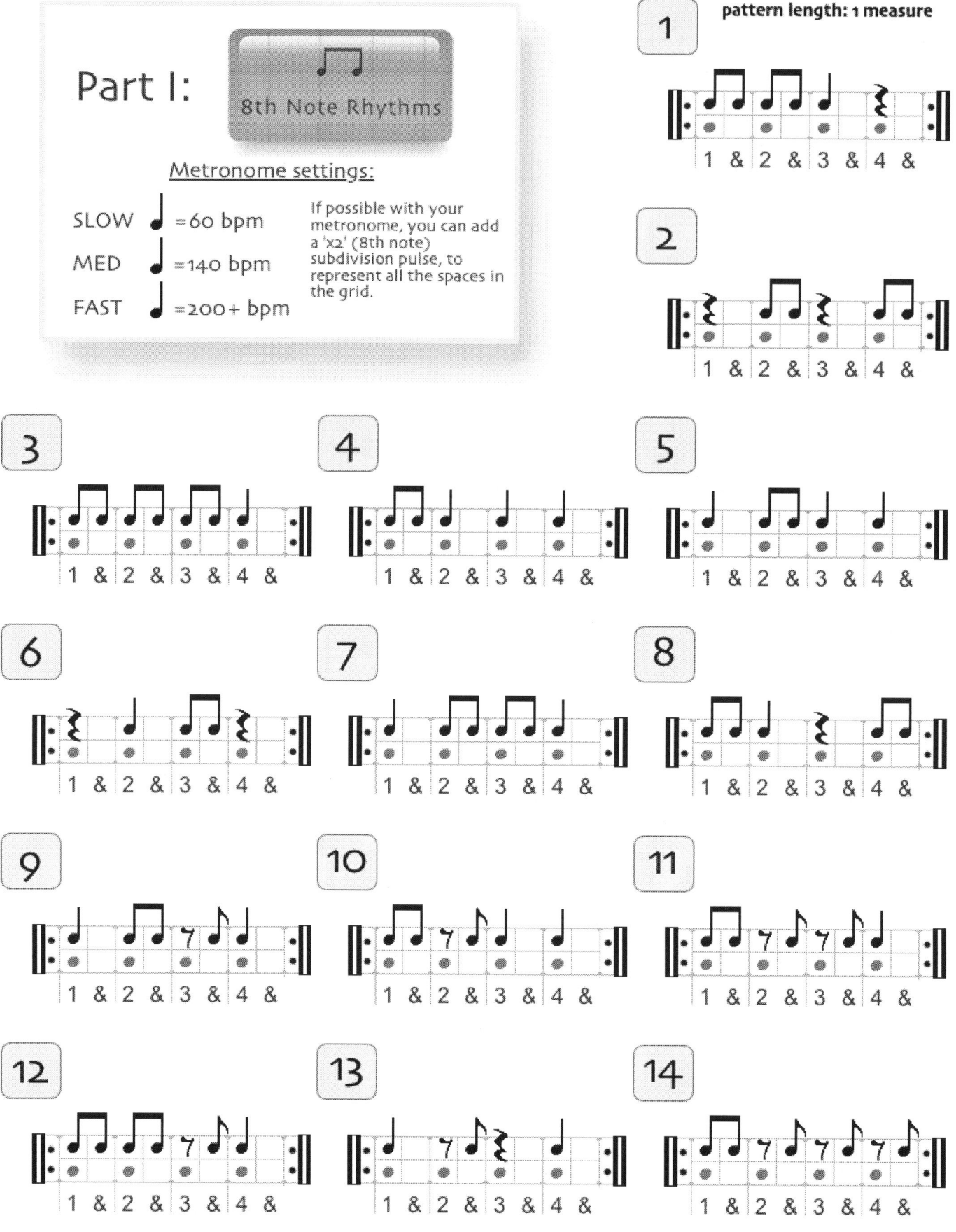

UNIVERSAL RHYTHMS part I - 8th Note Feel

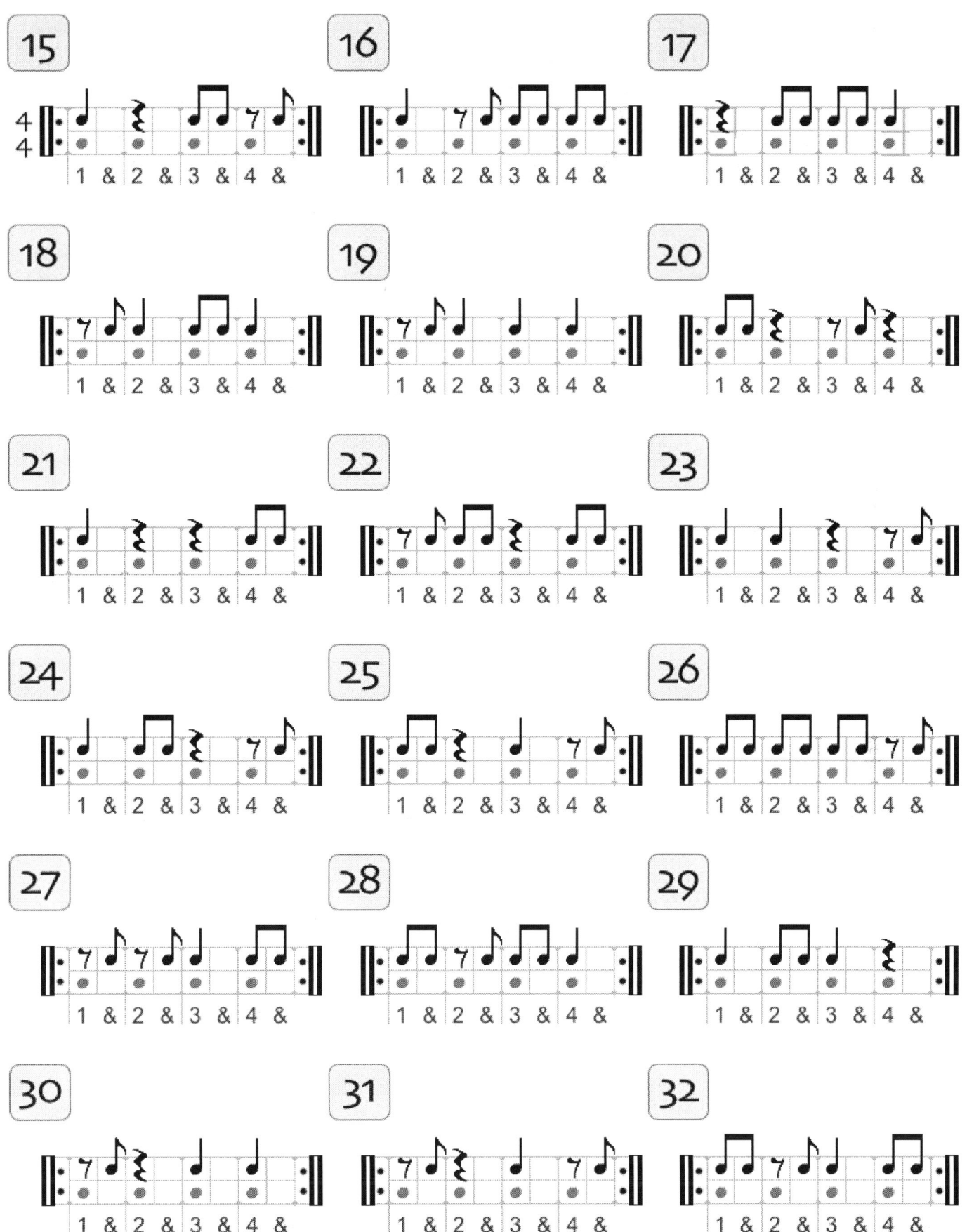

UNIVERSAL RHYTHMS part I - 8th Note Feel

UNIVERSAL RHYTHMS
PART II:
8th Triplet Feel

- 1+2 BEAT LENGTH RHYTHMS - P.27
- 1-MEASURE LENGTH RHYTHMS - P.28
- 4-MEASURE LENGTH RHYTHMS - P.30

(Full rhythm instructions on p.20)

Part II: 8th Triplet FEEL

Metronome settings:

SLOW ♩ =50 bpm

MED ♩ =120 bpm

FAST ♩ =190+ bpm

If possible with your metronome, you can add a 'x3' (8th triplet) subdivision pulse, to represent all the spaces in the grid.

pattern length: 1 beat

1

2

3

4

5

6

7

pattern length: 2 beats

8

9

10

11

12

13

14

15

16

17

18

19

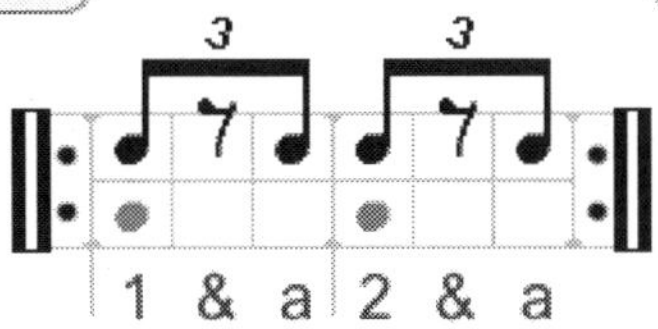

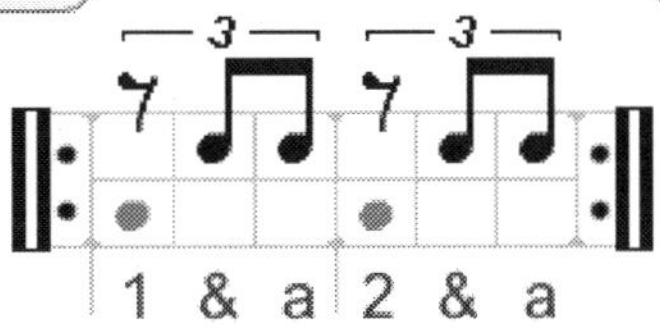

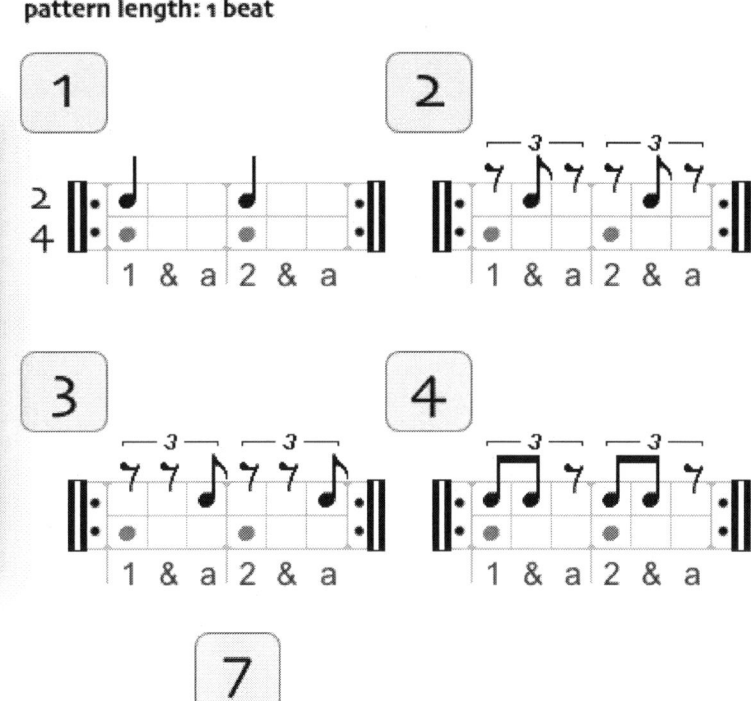

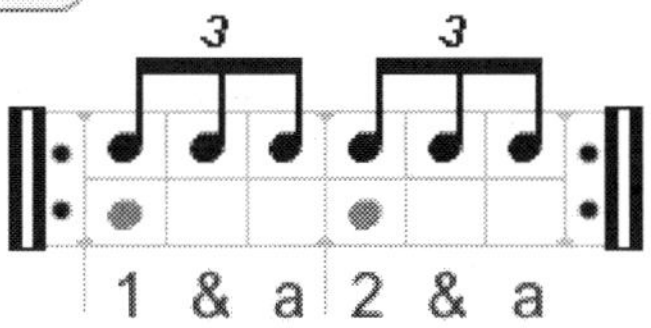

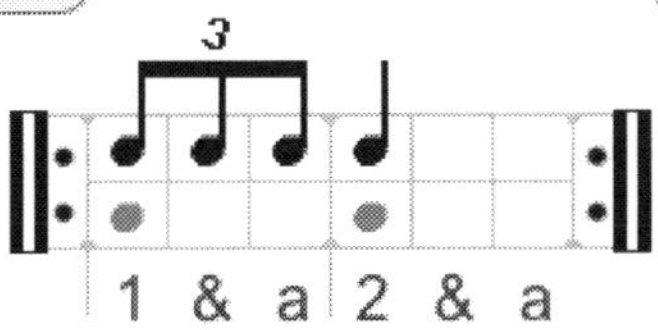

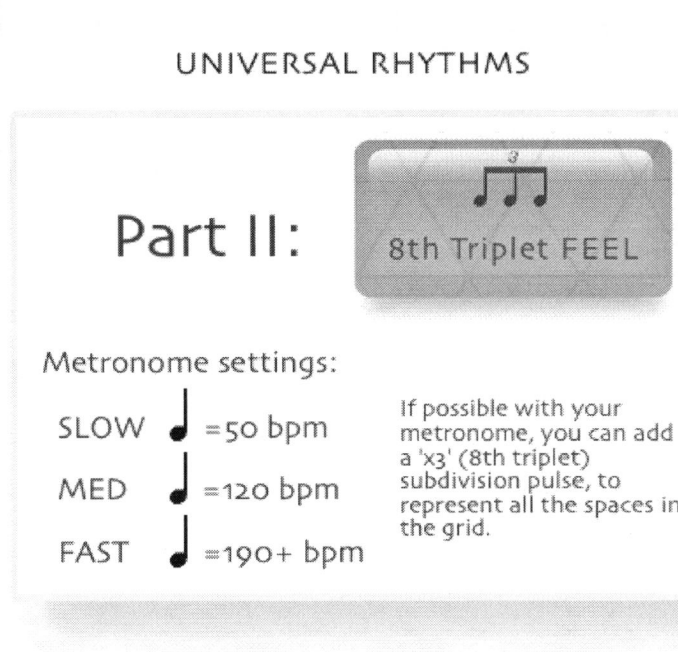

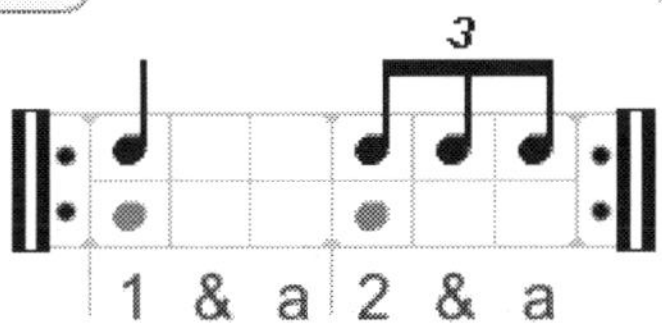

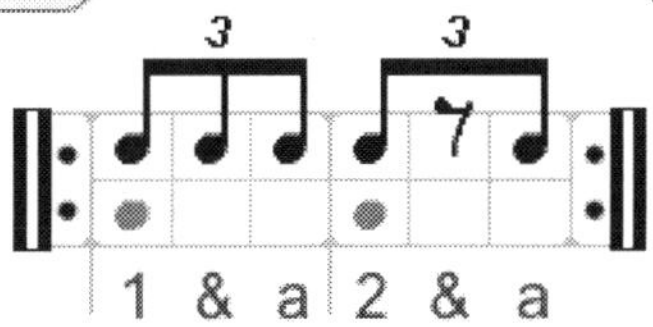

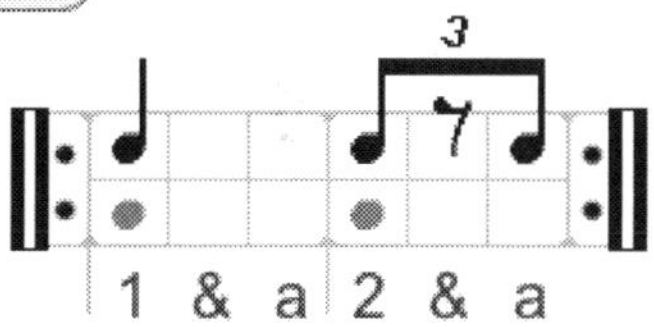

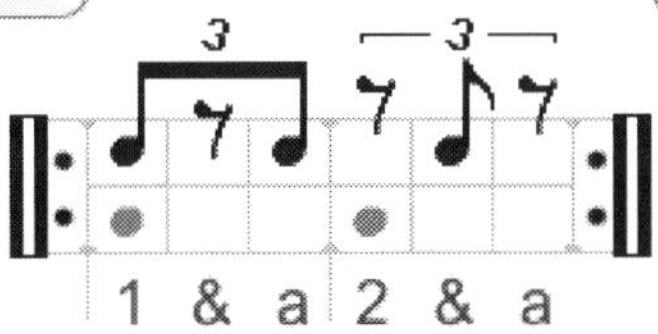

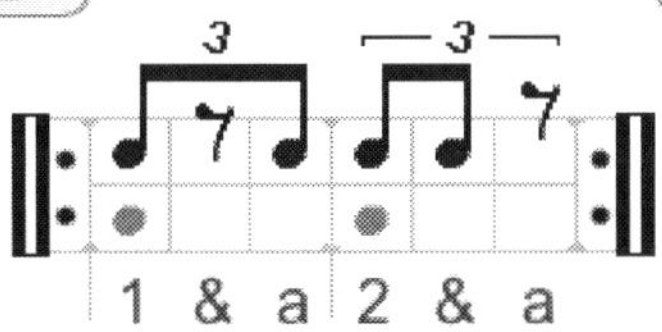

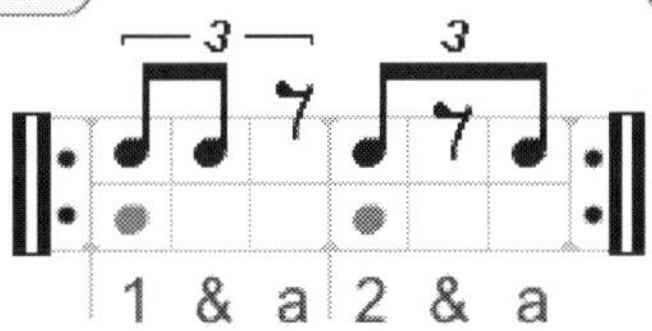

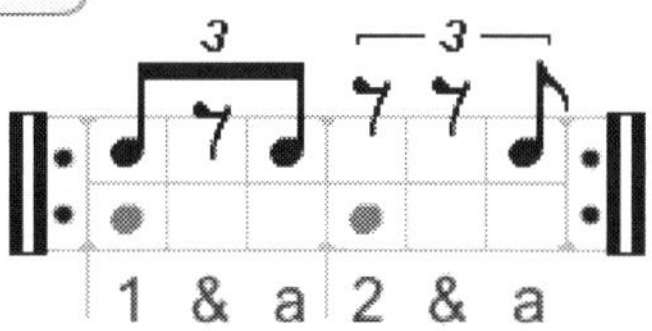

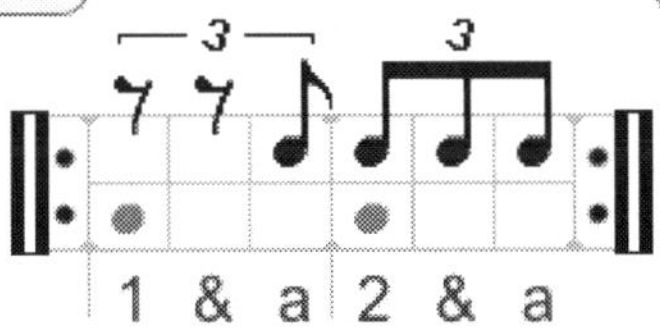

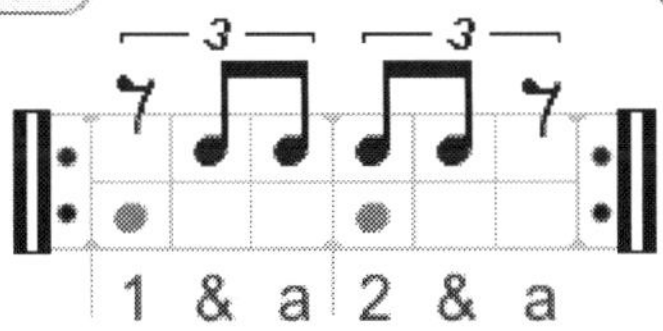

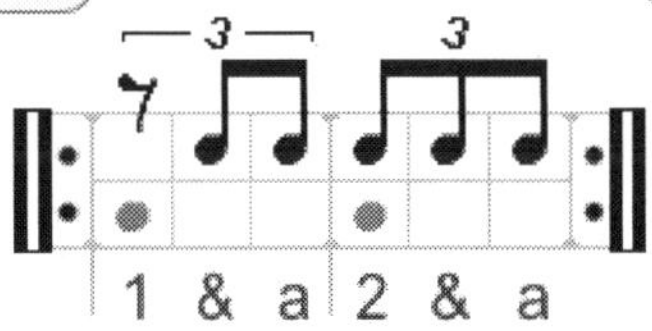

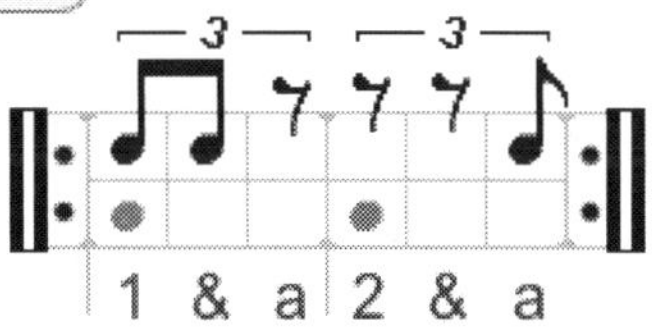

UNIVERSAL RHYTHMS part II - 8th Triplet Feel

UNIVERSAL RHYTHMS part II - 8th Triplet Feel

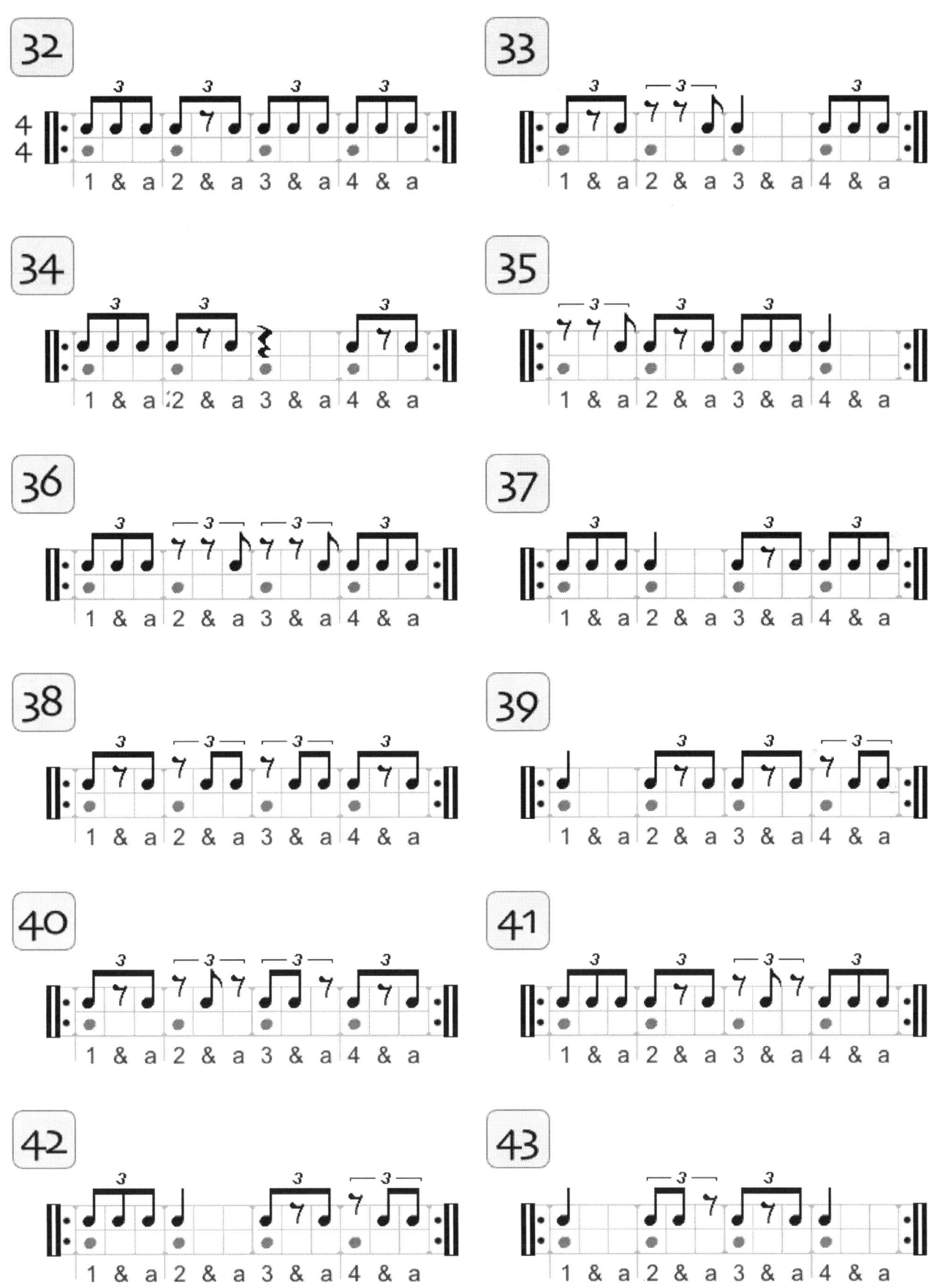

UNIVERSAL RHYTHMS part II - 8th Triplet Feel

44 pattern length: 4 measures

30

UNIVERSAL RHYTHMS part II - 8th Triplet Feel

The following section has some of the most commonly used rhythm notation, so practice this section a lot to make sure you're comfortable reading these rhythms!

UNIVERSAL RHYTHMS
PART III:
16th Note Feel

- 1 BEAT LENGTH RHYTHMS - P.34
- 2-BEAT LENGTH RHYTHMS - P.35
- 1-MEASURE LENGTH RHYTHMS - P.36
- 4-MEASURE LENGTH RHYTHMS - P.38

(Full rhythm instructions on p.20)

UNIVERSAL RHYTHMS

Part III: 16th Note FEEL

Metronome settings:

SLOW ♩ =80 bpm
MED ♩ =110 bpm
FAST ♩ =140+ bpm

If possible with your metronome, you can add a 'x2' (8th note) subdivision pulse, or a 'x4' (16th note) pulse to represent all the spaces in the grid.

pattern length: 1 beat

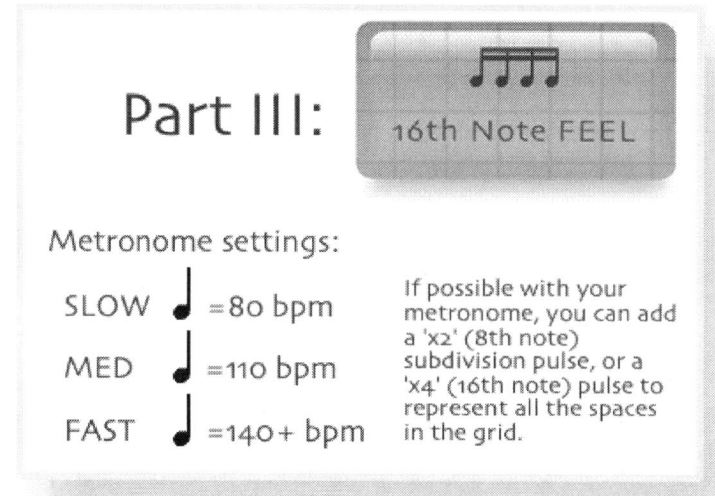

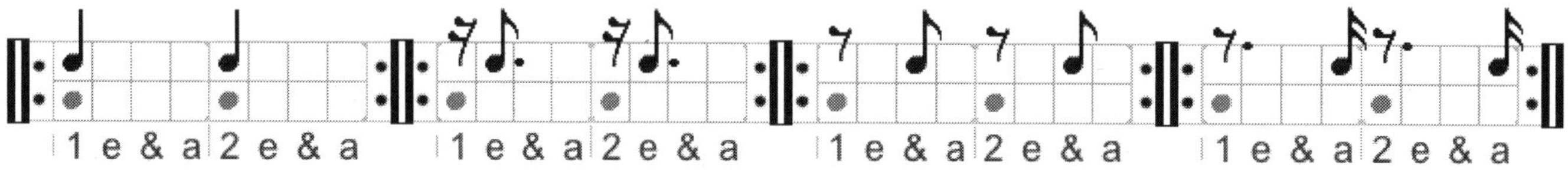

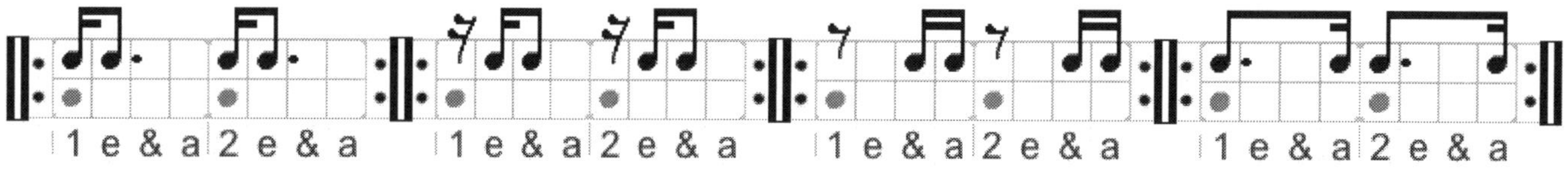

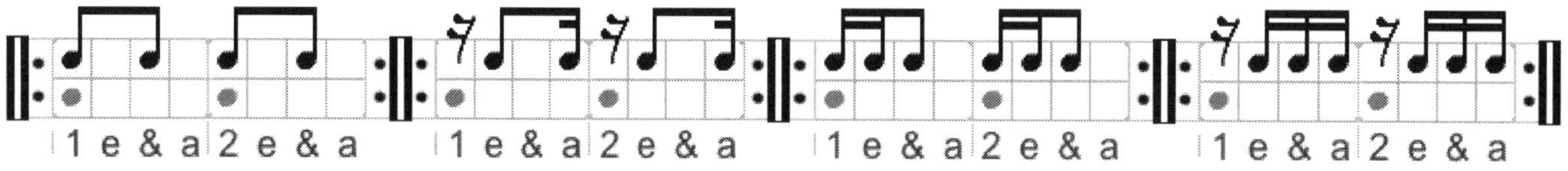

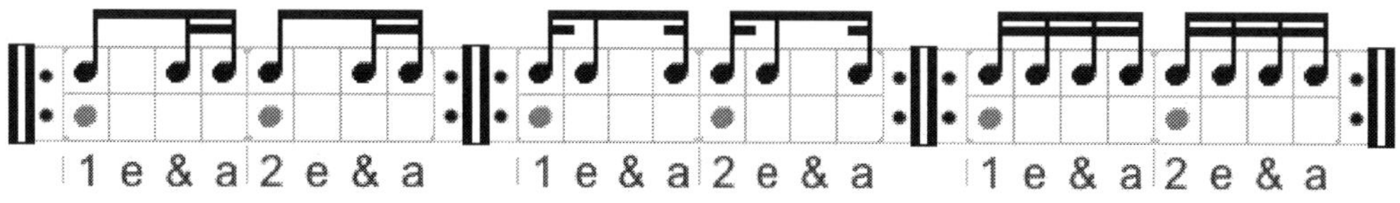

UNIVERSAL RHYTHMS part III - 16th Note Feel

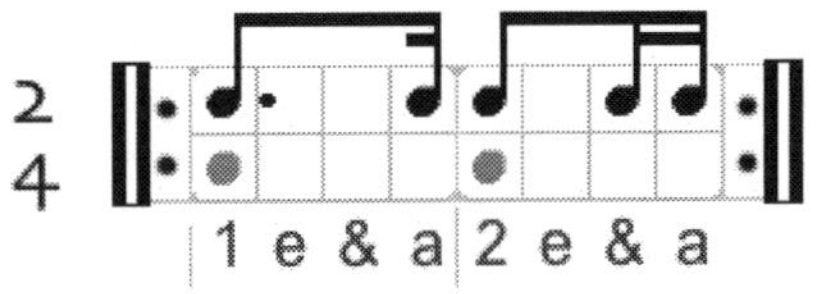

pattern length: 2 beats

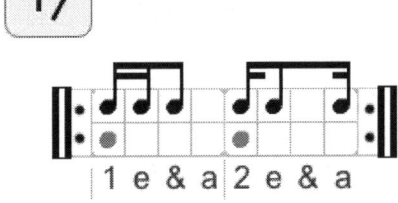
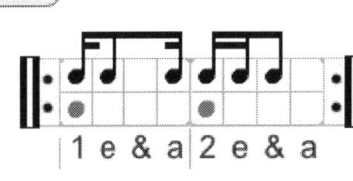
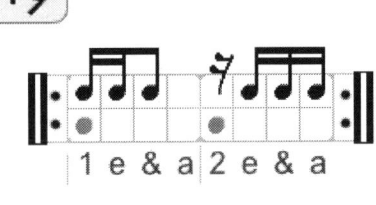
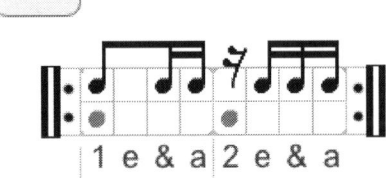
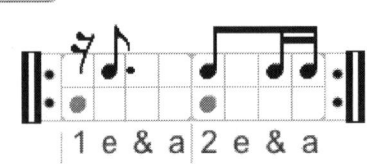
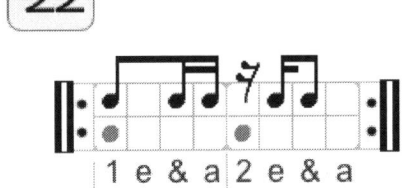
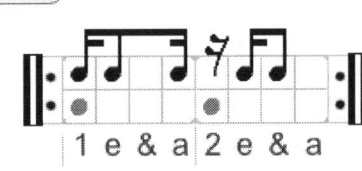
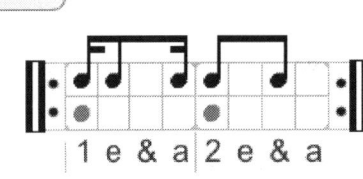
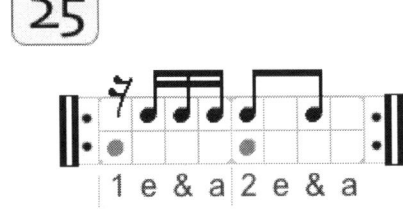
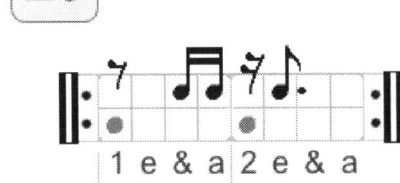
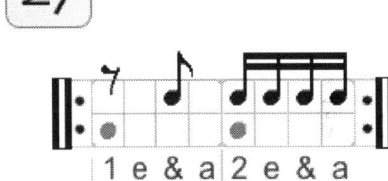
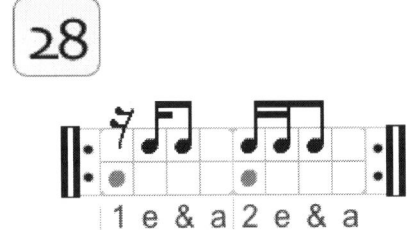
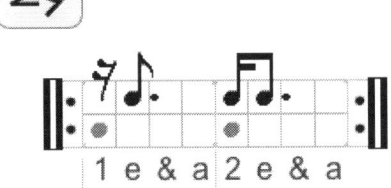
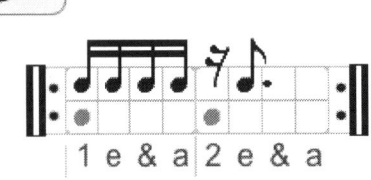
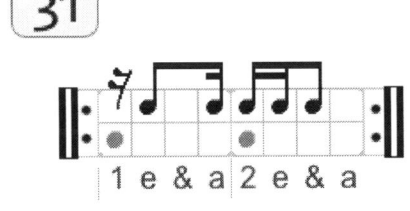
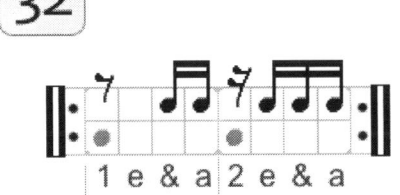
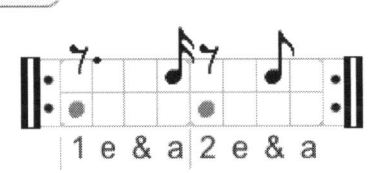

UNIVERSAL RHYTHMS part III - 16th Note Feel

pattern length: 1 measure

34
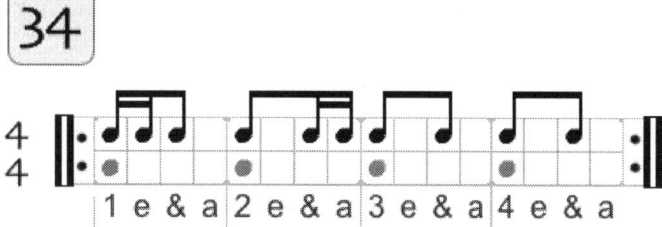

35
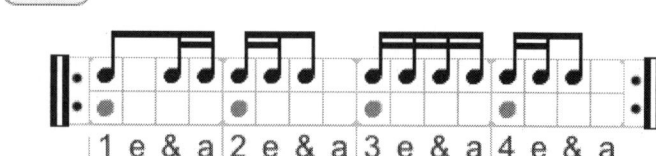

36
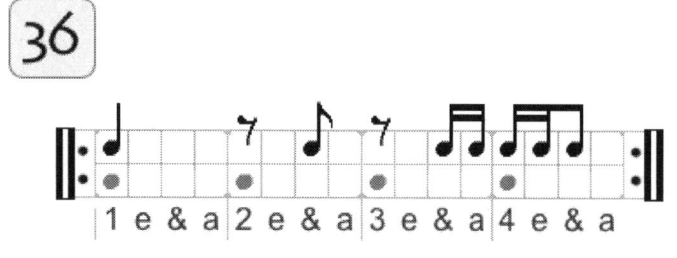

37
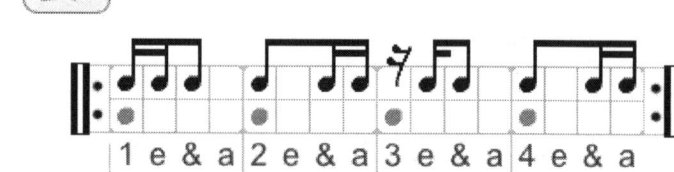

38
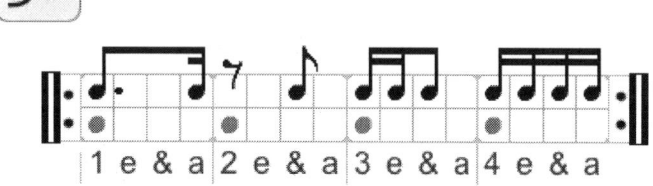

39
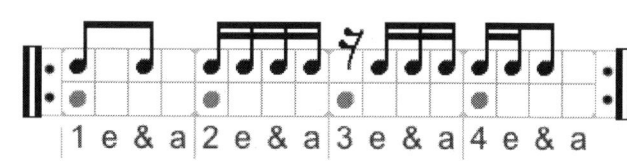

40
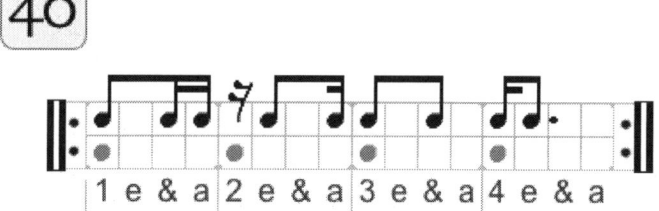

41
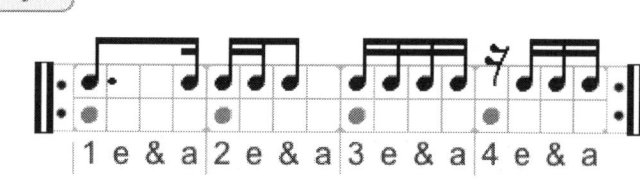

42
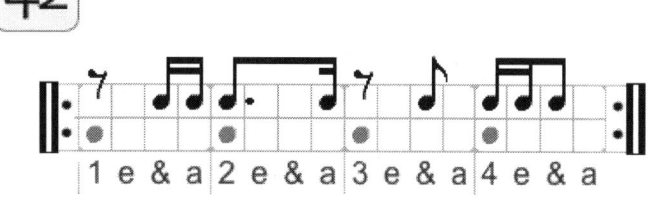

43
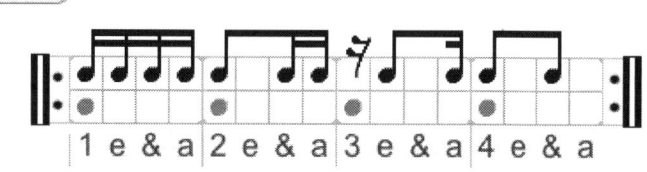

44
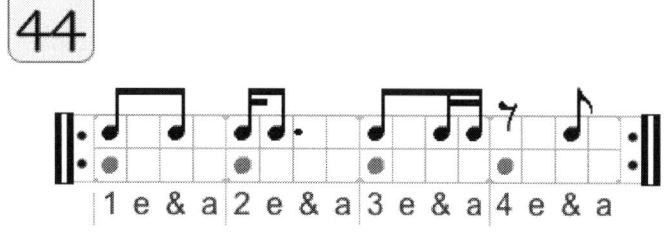

45
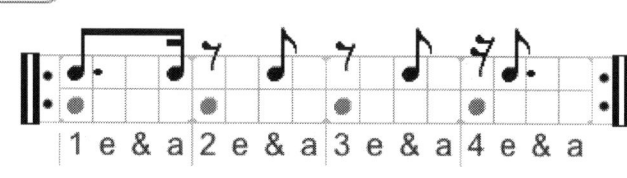

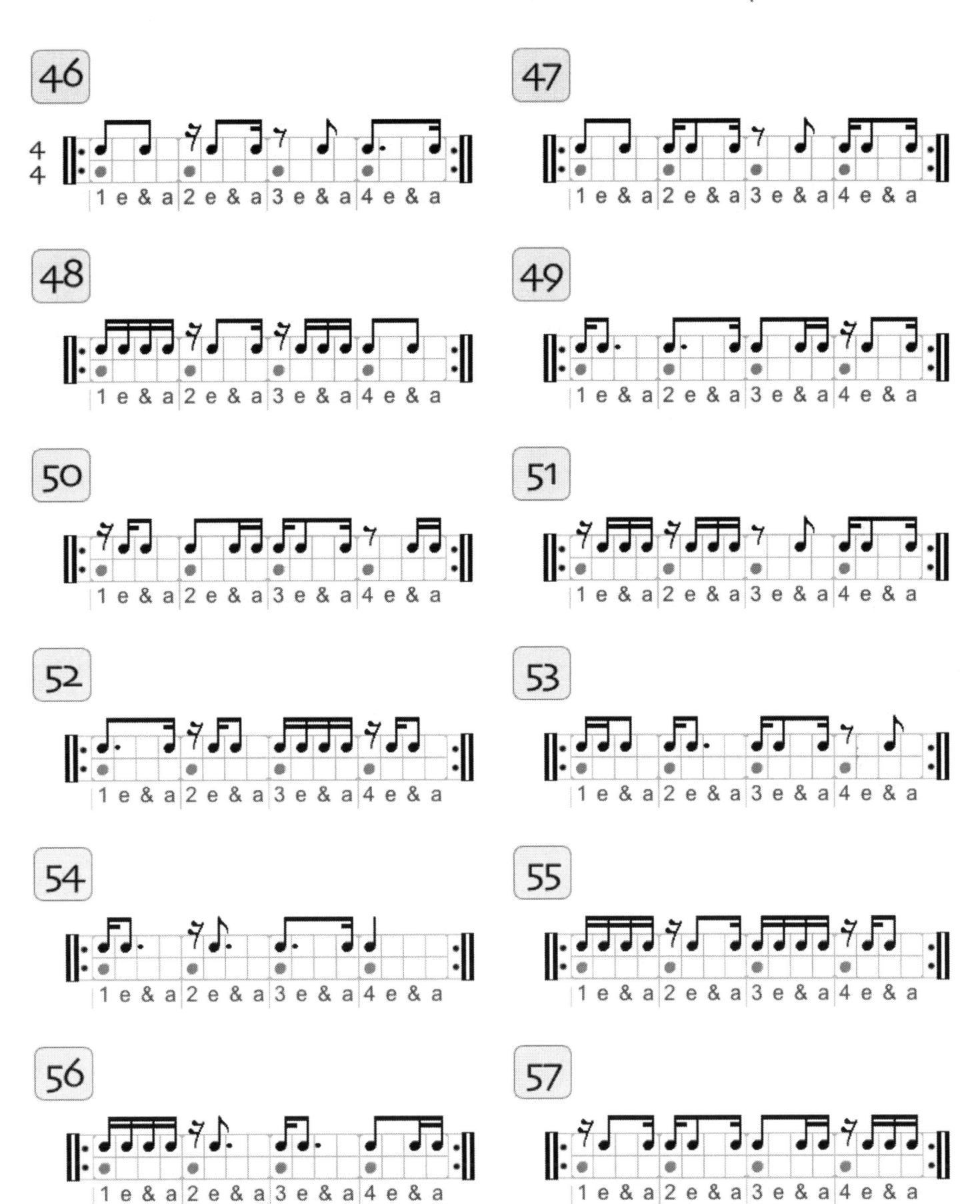

UNIVERSAL RHYTHMS part III - 16th Note Feel

UNIVERSAL RHYTHMS part III - 16th Note Feel

58 pattern length: 4 measures

1 e & a 2 e & a 3 e & a 4 e & a

59

60

61

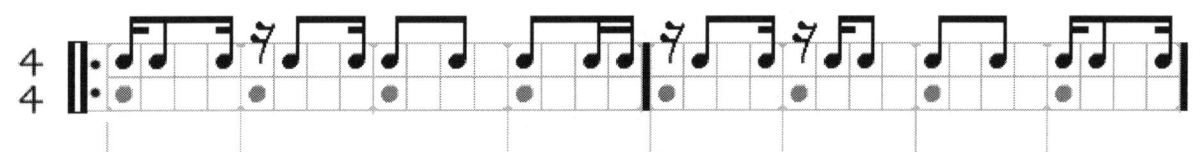

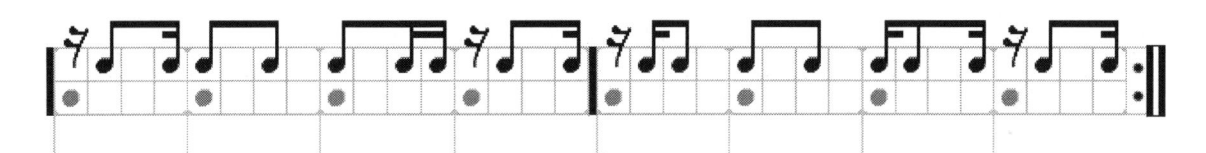

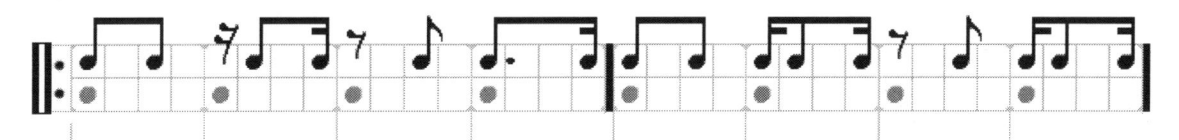

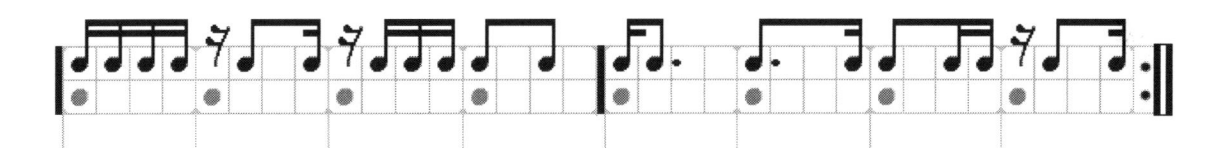

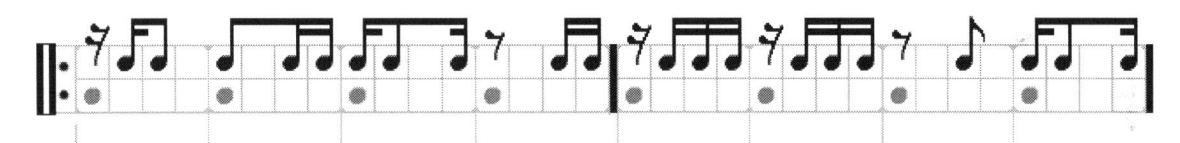

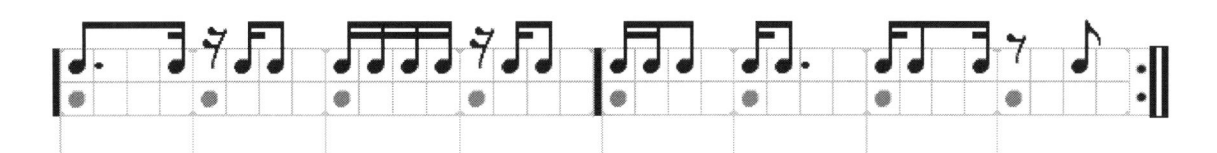

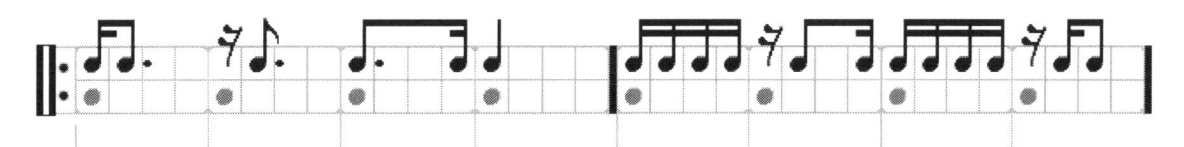

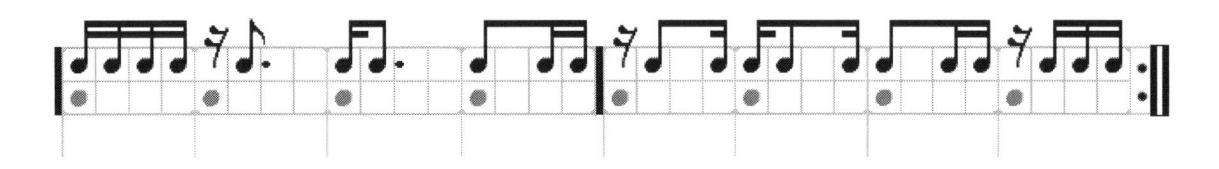

UNIVERSAL RHYTHMS part III - 16th Note Feel

UNIVERSAL RHYTHMS
PART IV:
6/8 Time Feel

6/8 Time FEEL

- 3-BEAT LENGTH RHYTHMS - P.41

- 1-MEASURE LENGTH RHYTHMS - P.42

- 4-MEASURE LENGTH RHYTHMS - P.44

(Full rhythm instructions on p.20)

PLAY DRUMS NOW
THE ULTIMATE DRUMSET TRAINING PROGRAM

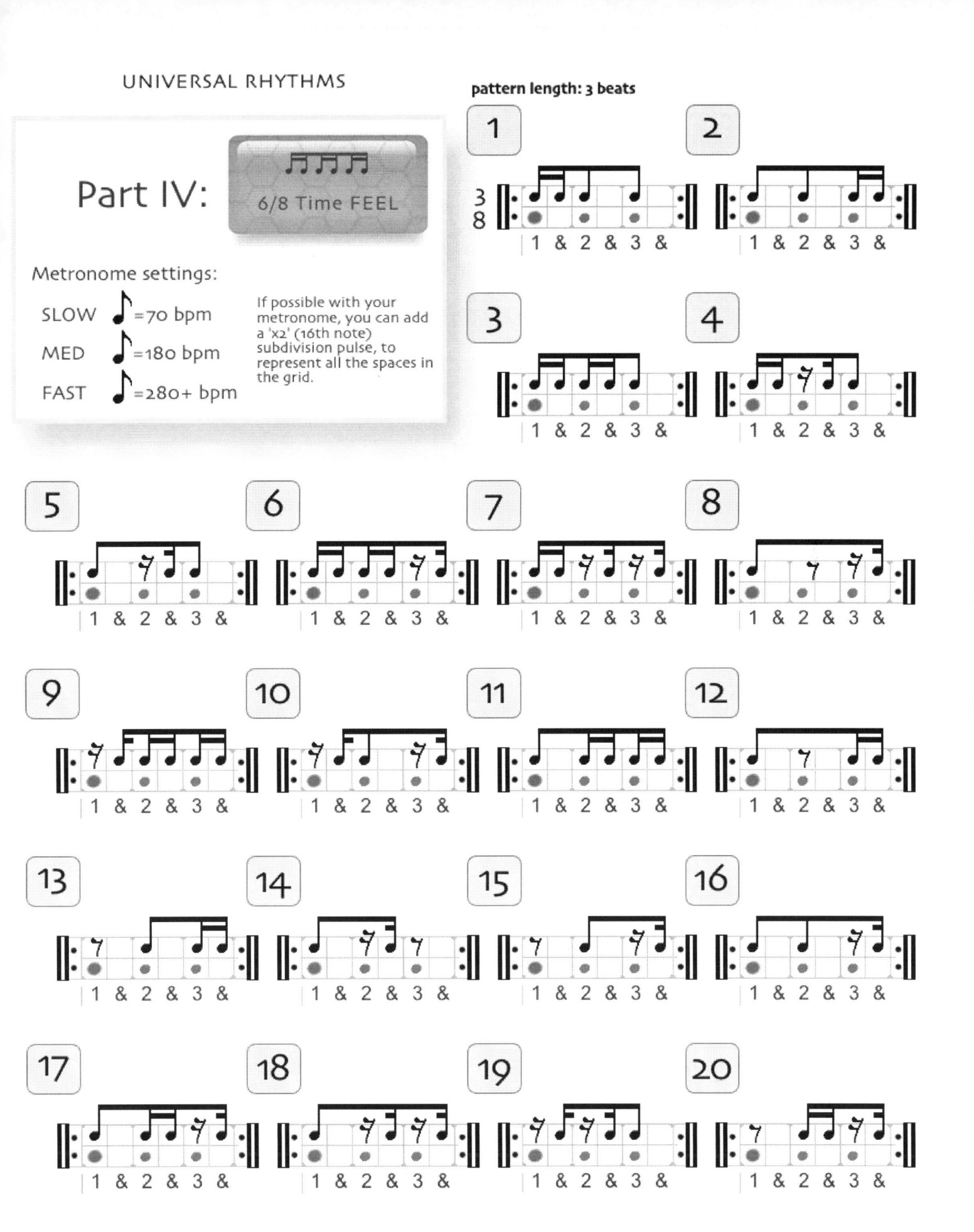

UNIVERSAL RHYTHMS

Part IV: 6/8 Time FEEL

Metronome settings:

- SLOW ♪ = 70 bpm
- MED ♪ = 180 bpm
- FAST ♪ = 280+ bpm

If possible with your metronome, you can add a 'x2' (16th note) subdivision pulse, to represent all the spaces in the grid.

pattern length: 3 beats

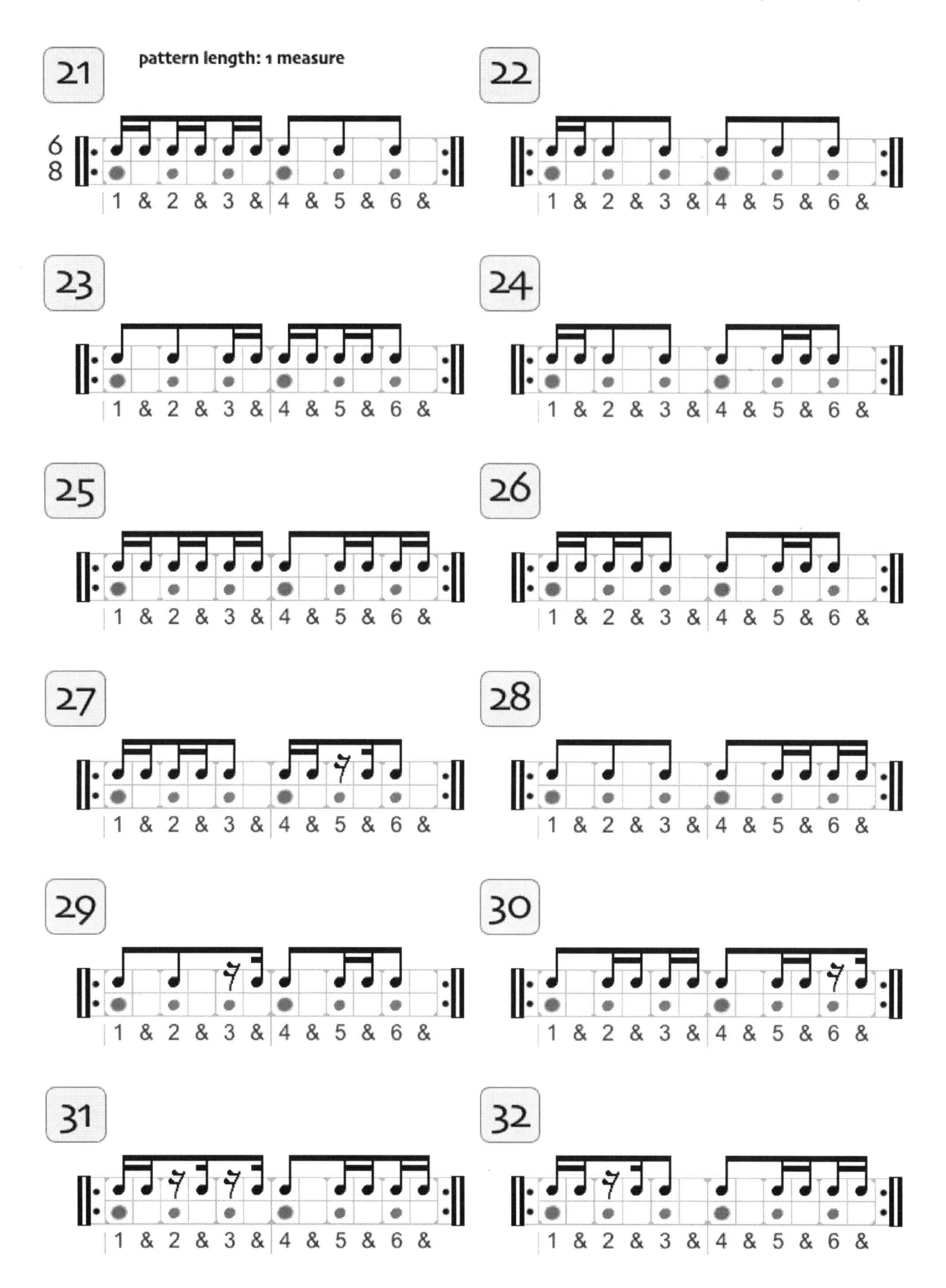

UNIVERSAL RHYTHMS part IV - 6/8 Time Feel

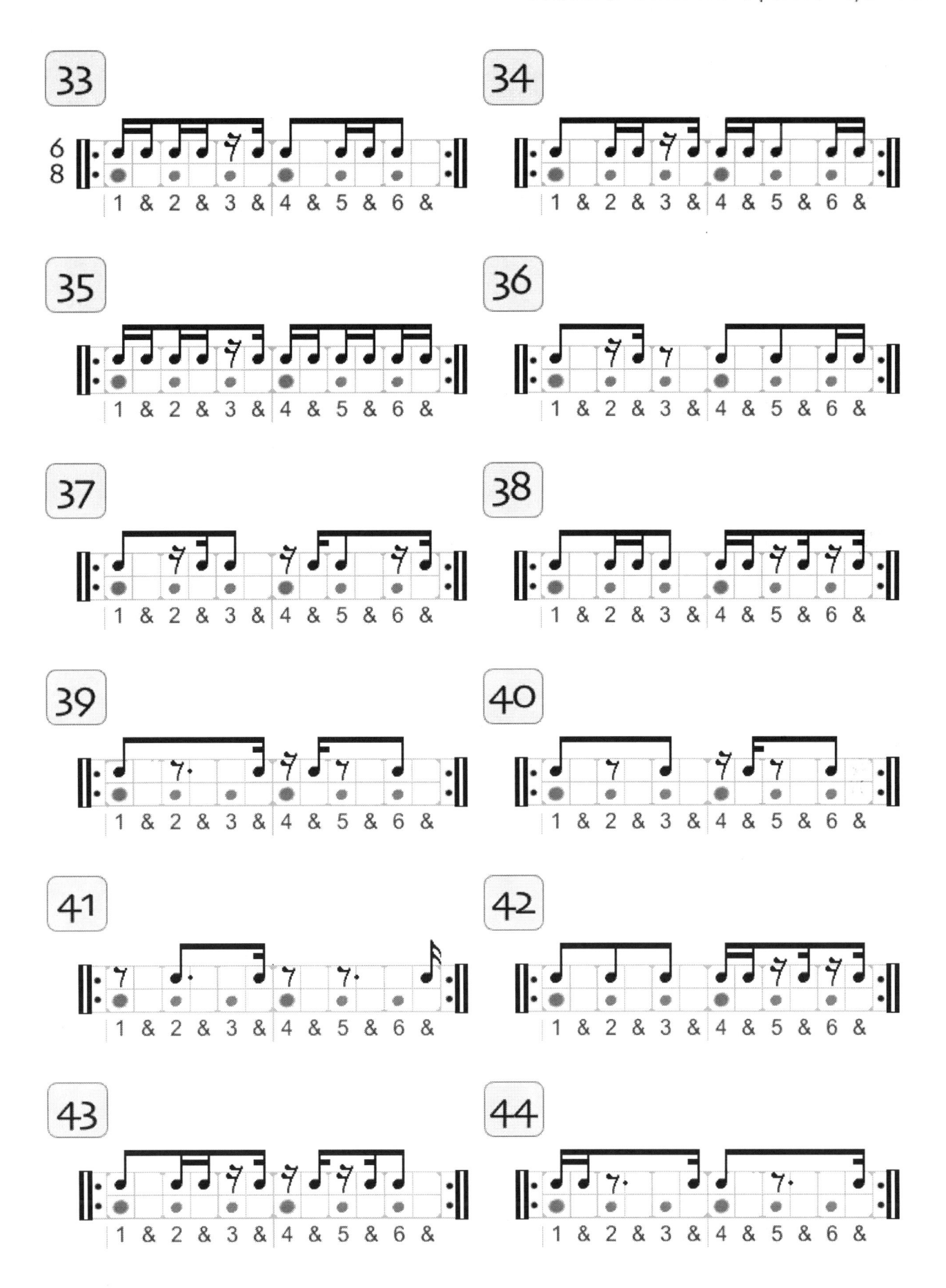

UNIVERSAL RHYTHMS part IV - 6/8 Time Feel

UNIVERSAL RHYTHMS part IV - 6/8 Time Feel

45 pattern length: 4 measures

6/8 | 1 & 2 & 3 & 4 & 5 & 6 &

46

47

48

44

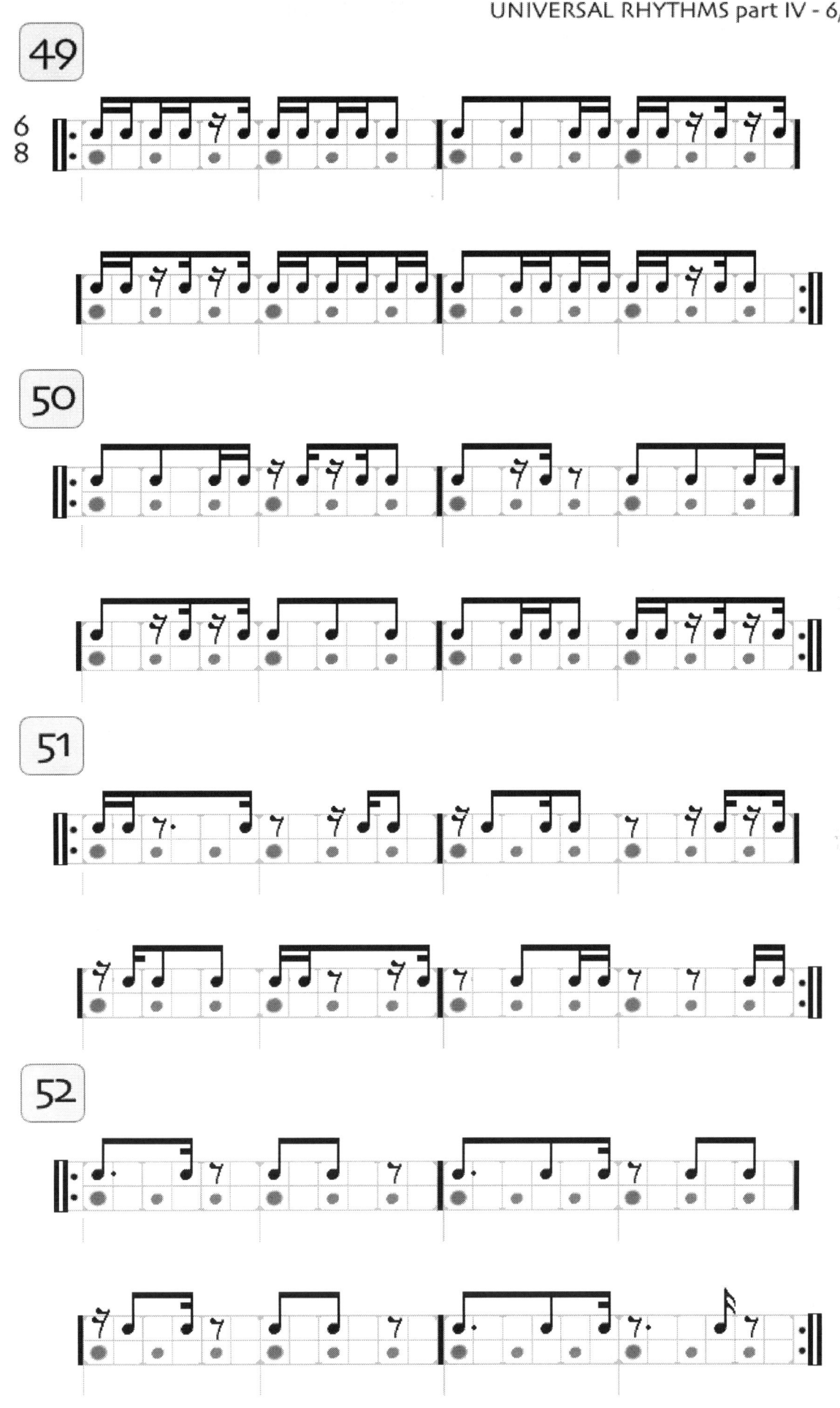

UNIVERSAL RHYTHMS part IV - 6/8 Time Feel

UNIVERSAL RHYTHMS
PART V:
16th Triplet Feel

- **2-BEAT LENGTH RHYTHMS - P.47**
- **1-MEASURE LENGTH RHYTHMS - P.48**

(Full rhythm instructions on p.20)

PLAY DRUMS NOW
THE ULTIMATE DRUMSET TRAINING PROGRAM

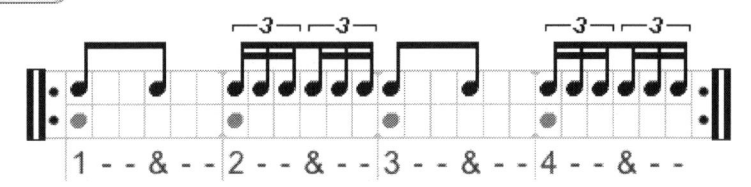

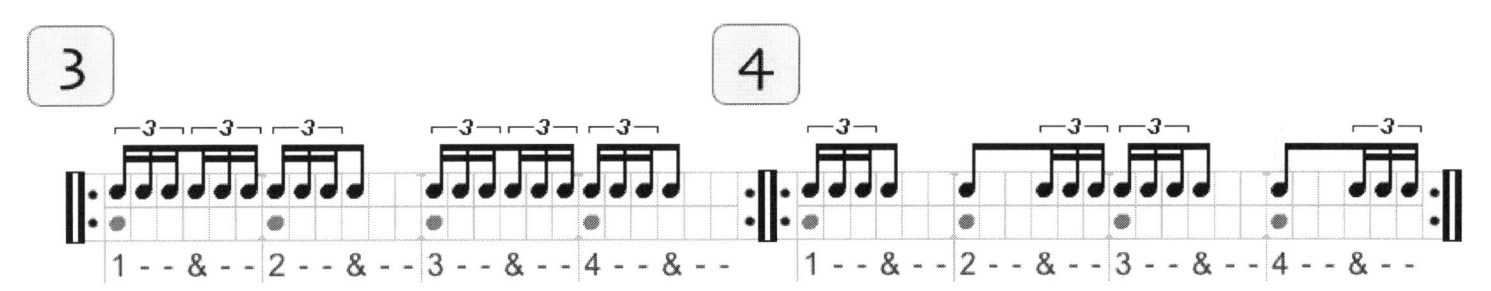

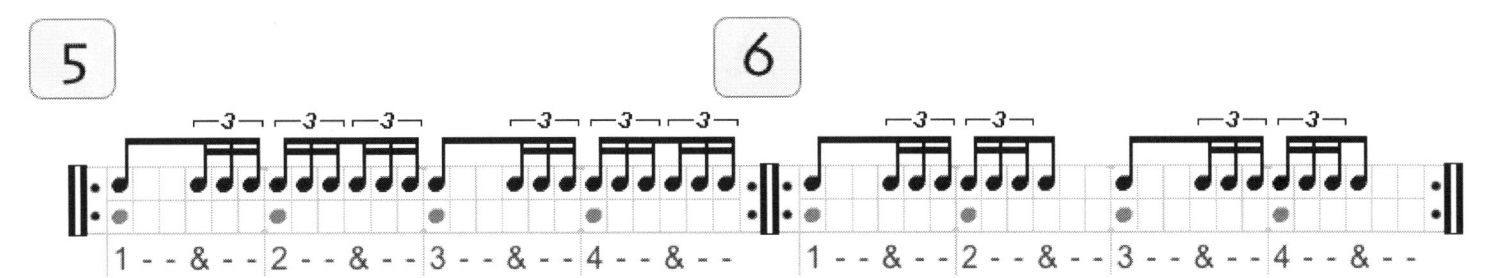

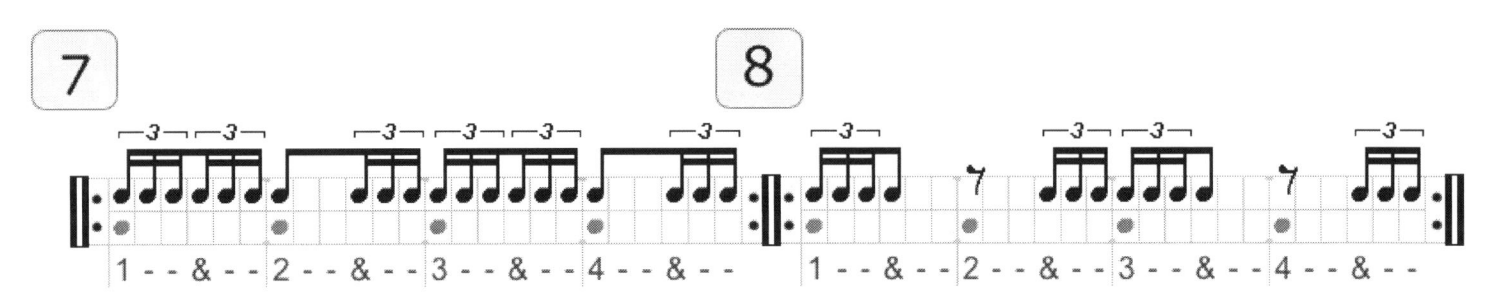

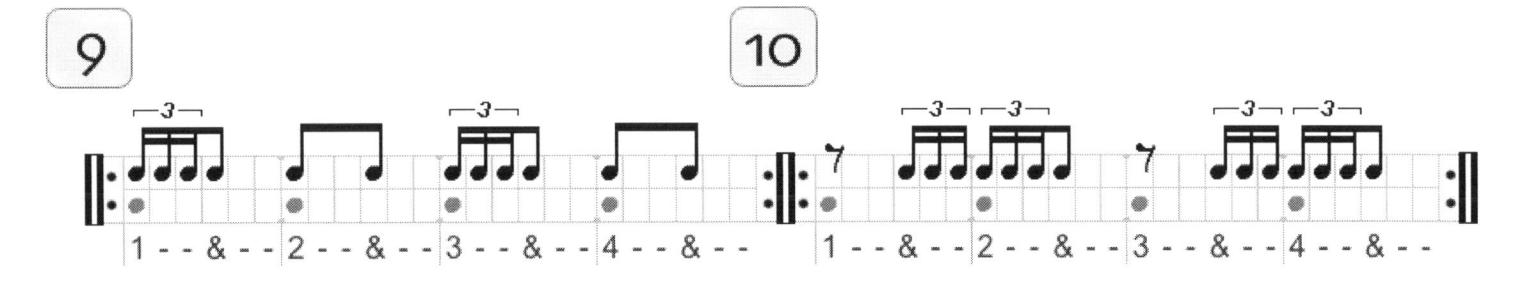

UNIVERSAL RHYTHMS

Part V: 16th Triplet FEEL

Metronome settings:

SLOW ♩ = 50 bpm
MED ♩ = 80 bpm
FAST ♩ = 110+ bpm

If possible with your metronome, you can add a 'x2' (8th note) subdivision pulse, or a 'x6' (16th triplet) pulse to represent all the spaces in the grid.

pattern length: 1/2 measure

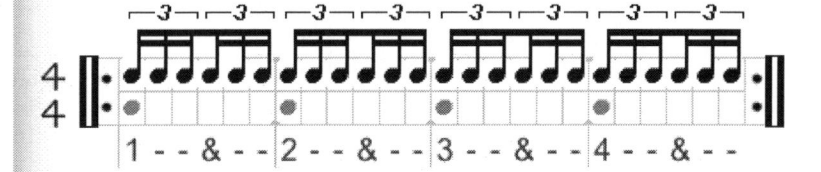

UNIVERSAL RHYTHMS part V - 16th Triplet Feel

UNIVERSAL RHYTHMS
PART VI:

Swung 16th Feel

Swung 16th FEEL

This is an important adaptation to the '16th Note Feel'. **Play all those rhythms again,** with the 'swing modification' (see following pages).

- 16TH NOTE FEEL RHYTHMS - P.34

(Full rhythm instructions on p.20)

PLAY DRUMS NOW
THE ULTIMATE DRUMSET TRAINING PROGRAM

Part VI: Swung 16th FEEL

Metronome settings:

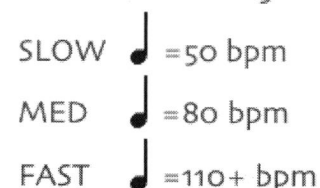

SLOW ♩ =50 bpm
MED ♩ =80 bpm
FAST ♩ =110+ bpm

If possible with your metronome, you can add a 'x2' (8th note) subdivision pulse, or a 'x6' (16th triplet) pulse to represent all the spaces in the grid.

To learn rhythms in the 'Swung 16th Feel', read/play the '16th Feel' rhythms again, and adjust the timing as shown below.

(Check out the song examples in the 'DRUMS Swung 16th Feel' Spotify playlist for clarity.)

16th Note Feel

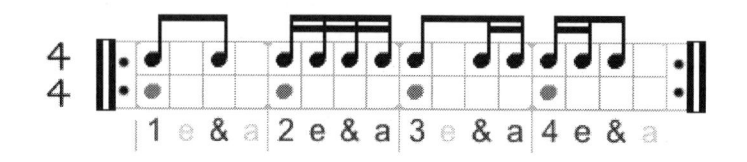

|1 e & a 2 e & a 3 e & a 4 e & a

Swung 16th Note Feel

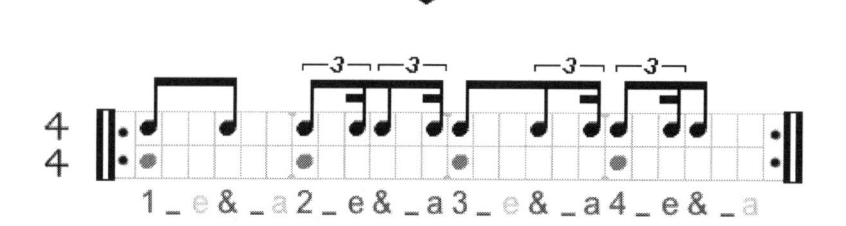

1 _ e & _ a 2 _ e & _ a 3 _ e & _ a 4 _ e & _ a

When counting vocally, instead of the steady sounding '1,e,&,a,2,e,&,a' it will sound more like
'1 - e,& - a,2 - e,& - a'.

To 'swing' a 16th note pattern, each pair of 16th note counts gets widened, adding a space to the middle. The result is a rhythm that lines up with the first and third notes of triplets, but never uses the middle note.

HERE ARE SOME PATTERNS TO GET YOU STARTED:

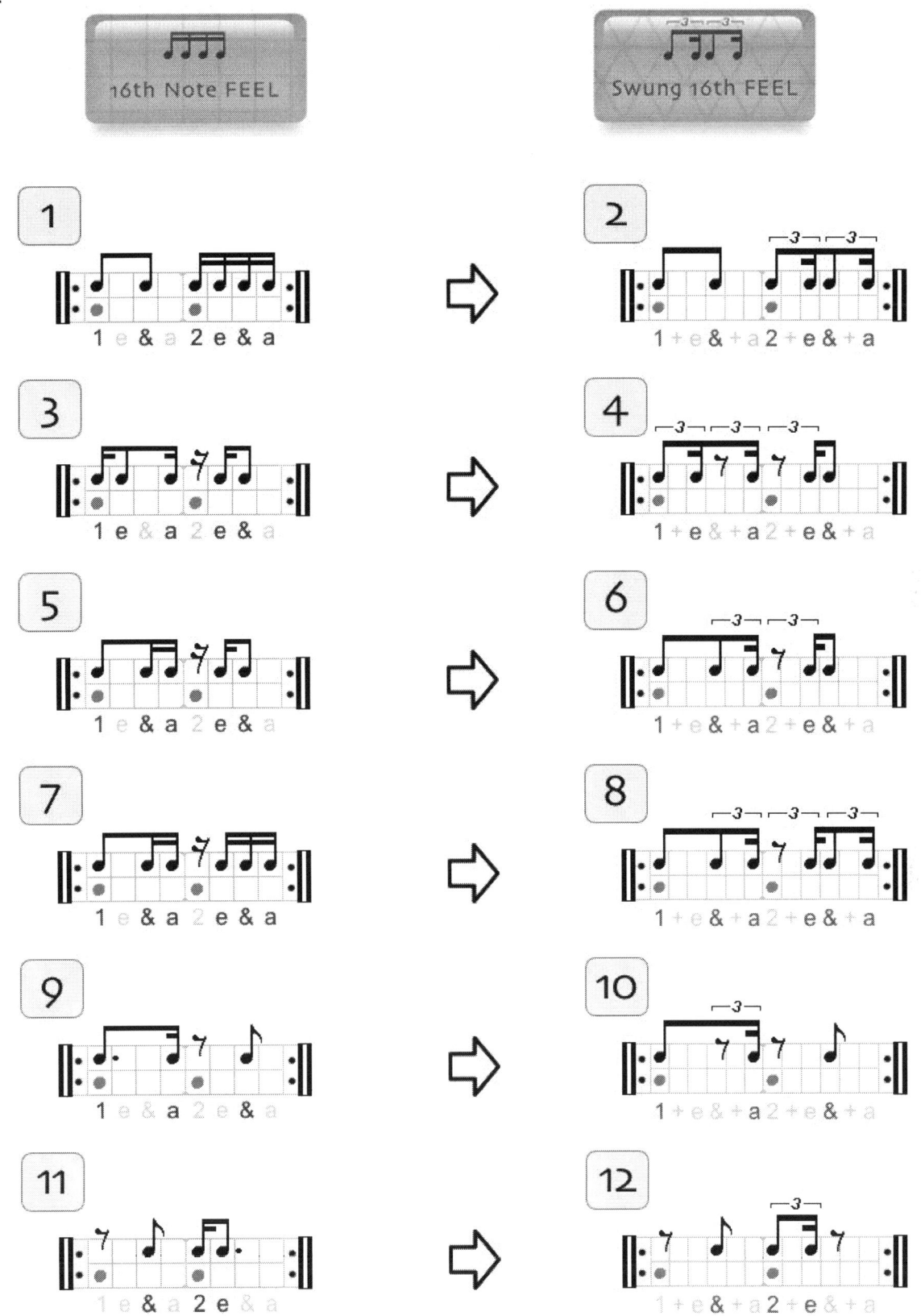

16th Note FEEL → **Swung 16th FEEL**

NOW RETURN TO PAGES 34-39 AND PLAY THOSE EXERCISES WITH A 'SWING FEEL'.

UNIVERSAL RHYTHMS
PART VII:
32nd Note Feel

- **1-MEASURE LENGTH RHYTHMS – P.53**

    (Full rhythm instructions on p.20)

UNIVERSAL RHYTHMS

Part VII: 32nd Note Rhythms

Metronome settings:

SLOW ♩ = 30 bpm
MED ♩ = 60 bpm
FAST ♩ = 100+ bpm

If possible with your metronome, you can add a 'x4' (16th note) or a 'x8' (32nd note) subdivision pulse.

1
1-e-&-a-2-e-&-a-3-e-&-a-4-e-&-a-

2
1-e-&-a-2-e-&-a-3-e-&-a-4-e-&-a-

3
1-e-&-a-2-e-&-a-3-e-&-a-4-e-&-a-

4
1-e-&-a-2-e-&-a-3-e-&-a-4-e-&-a-

5
1-e-&-a-2-e-&-a-3-e-&-a-4-e-&-a-

6
1-e-&-a-2-e-&-a-3-e-&-a-4-e-&-a-

7
1-e-&-a-2-e-&-a-3-e-&-a-4-e-&-a-

8
1-e-&-a-2-e-&-a-3-e-&-a-4-e-&-a-

9
1-e-&-a-2-e-&-a-3-e-&-a-4-e-&-a-

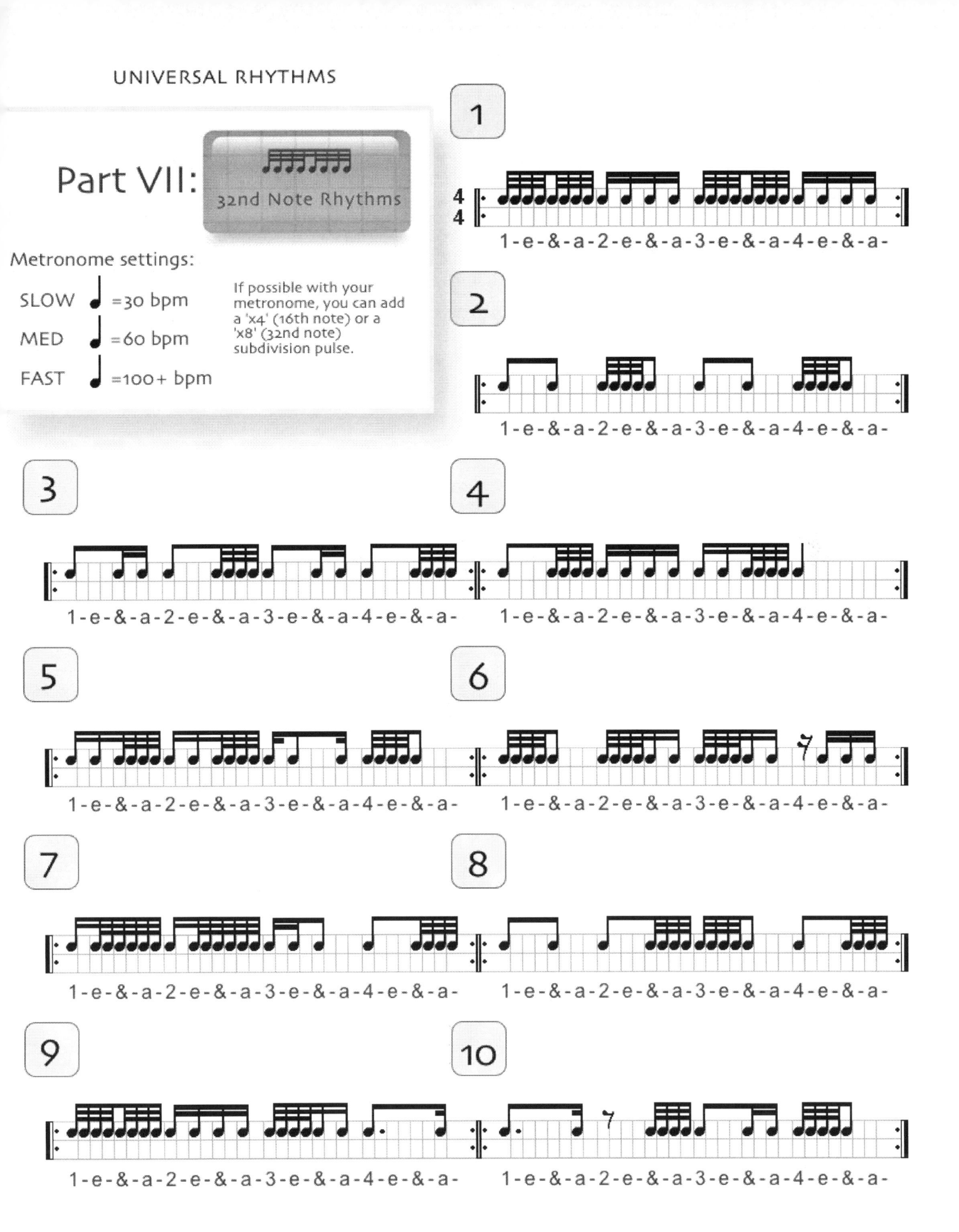

10
1-e-&-a-2-e-&-a-3-e-&-a-4-e-&-a-

UNIVERSAL RHYTHMS part VII - 32nd Note Rhythms

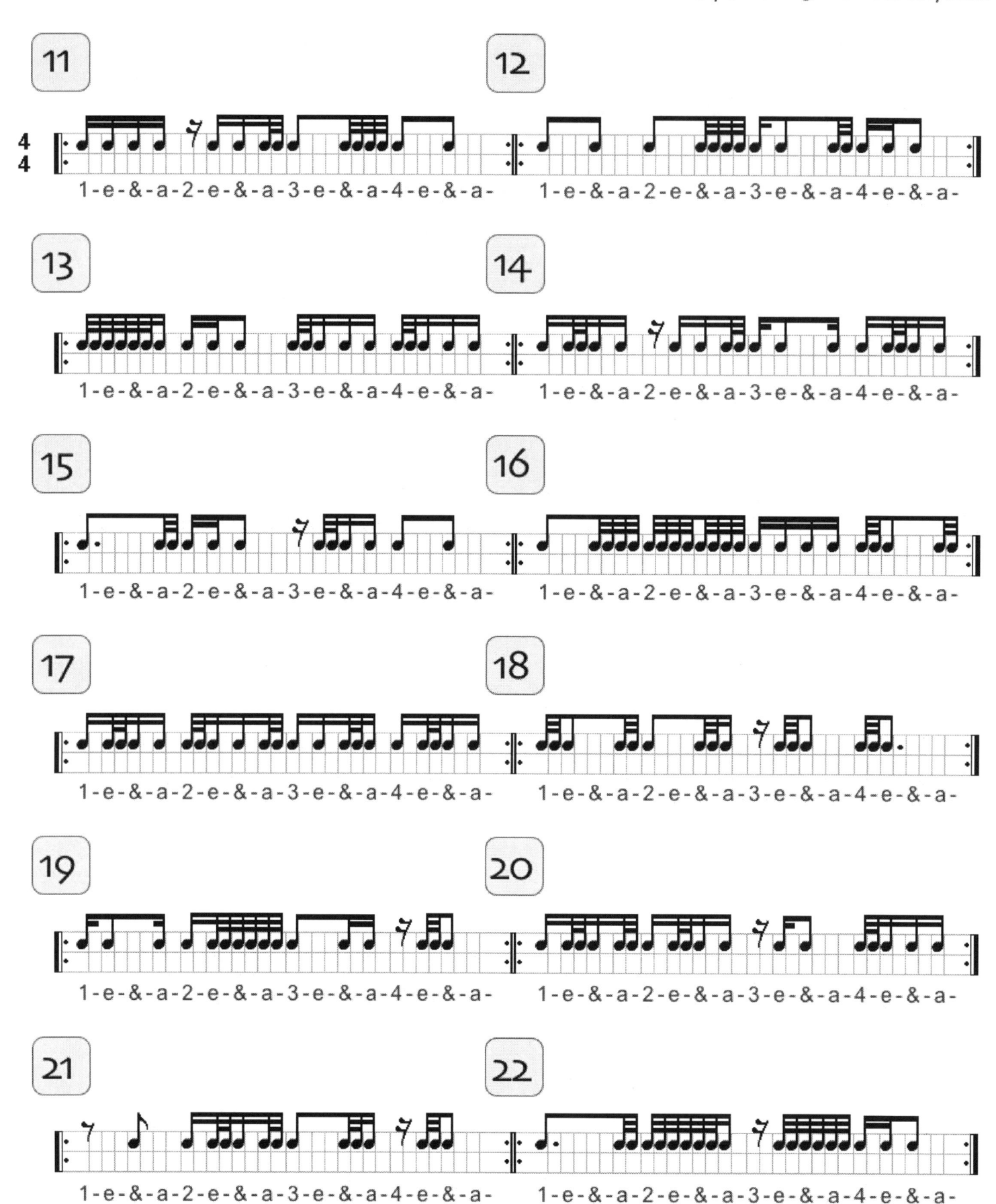

Did you complete this book?

CONGRATS!!!

NICE WORK.

SKILLS ASSESSMENT:

Check these criteria to see if you're ready to move on from this book!

- You understand the knowledge and wisdom in the written sections of this book
- You have experienced an increase in skill from training with this material
- You can play any of the exercises in this book at a comfortable tempo
- You feel confident in your ability to learn and play new similar material
- You are motivated to learn more and become a better drummer

NEXT STEPS:

- Continue to the next book in LEVEL 2: **'Play Drums Now 2.3: Drumset Grooves'**
- Go to www.PlayDrumsNow.com for more resources.

ABOUT THE AUTHOR:

Adam Randall - Drummer, educator, and author. Adam has performed and recorded drums professionally with bands across various styles. His career in drum instruction started with ten years at the Colorado Music Institute, and he has since been teaching at Klash Drums in MN. He published his first books on drum instruction in 2010, and he continues to create new materials as part of his mission to make it easier for people to become great drummers.

Follow @playdrumsnow on Instagram, facebook, twitter, youtube etc. for more!

WWW.PLAYDRUMSNOW.COM
ADAM RANDALL

GENERAL PRACTICE TIPS

PRACTICING IS IMPORTANT because your body has a **physical memory,** which is very different from (and learns a bit slower than) your cognitive memory. YOU MUST BE PATIENT while teaching yourself any physical pattern you want to play on the drums!

> **"The more times in a row you do something the same way, the more your body can remember the action without your conscious mind."**

Make sure to keep your 'PLAYING' and 'PRACTICING' separate, and spend time each week doing both. 'Playing' is good for having fun, but 'practicing' is what creates progress.

'PLAYING' is when you allow your drumming to be fun and expressive, maybe spontaneous and creative. It's when you are using drumming as a musical art form, or just simply enjoying doing stuff you already know how to do.

'PRACTICING' is when you repeat some unfamiliar action carefully, until it becomes easier and more familiar and you GAIN CONTROL. Also known as 'rehearsing'.

THE 'IDEAL PRACTICE METHOD'
for learning any pattern

1. Read and imagine the exercise.

Imagine what your body is about to do

2. Play one count at a time, slowly and in control - no mistakes!

At least four consecutive measures

3. Play / loop the exercise with correct timing / rhythm.

Keep tempo steady, and look away from the written music.

4. Explore various tempos.

Try playing faster than you think you can handle, you'll often be surprised!

5. Improve the pattern's quality and your physical actions to play it.

Listen to the exercise as you play it, and observe how it feels physically to play it.

HOW OFTEN TO PRACTICE?

CASUAL: 30 - 60 min per week

SERIOUS: 1-2 hours per week

PRO: 3+ hours per week

Printed in France by Amazon
Brétigny-sur-Orge, FR